"If you have obsessions and compulsions related to the fear of harm, you should have this book! Jon Hershfield has an engaging writing style and a keen understanding of this problem that he passes along to the reader. Most importantly, he pulls together scientifically supported interventions into a useful self-help format. The numerous illustrations and examples will help you implement these strategies and overcome your harm-related OCD symptoms."

—**Jonathan S. Abramowitz, PhD**, professor in the department
of psychology at the University of North Carolina (UNC) at
Chapel Hill, and director of the UNC Anxiety and Stress Clinic

"I have often thought of harming Jon, since I am jealous that he writes these really good books that I wish I had written instead of him. But I will sit with that thought and just be happy with the fact that I have a great reference to refer my patients and my students to when questions of Harm OCD arise in therapy and supervision. Good work, Jon. This book will be a great addition to the OCD literature. Just watch your back..."

—**Patrick B. McGrath, PhD**, assistant vice president and
residential services clinical director at AMITA Health,
Foglia Family Foundation Residential Treatment Center

"*Overcoming Harm OCD* is a remarkable contribution to the self-help literature on OCD. Hershfield has a masterful way of presenting complex concepts in an easy-to-understand manner and then linking them with effective therapeutic strategies. This book will be a valuable resource for individuals with Harm OCD, as well as applied practitioners who work with individuals with OCD or who simply want to learn more."

—**Eric Storch, PhD**, vice chair, professor, and McIngvale
Presidential Endowed Chair at the Menninger Department of
Psychiatry and Behavioral Sciences at Baylor College of Medicine

T0299670

"If you have Harm OCD, the best thing you can do is work with a skilled therapist trained in cognitive behavioral therapy (CBT) for OCD like Jon Hershfield. The next best thing is to use *Overcoming Harm OCD* to help yourself. If you do find a good therapist, they may recommend the book too; I know I will recommend it for my Harm OCD patients."

—**James Claiborn, PhD, ABPP, ACT**, psychologist specializing in OCD and related disorders, diplomate of the American Board of Professional Psychology in Counseling Psychology, diplomate and founding fellow of the Academy of Cognitive Therapy, and coauthor of *The Habit Change Workbook* and *The BDD Workbook*

"*Overcoming Harm OCD* is an invaluable resource for anyone afflicted by inexplicable violent thoughts that they are terrified of acting upon, even while realizing their fears are irrational. The author, OCD therapist Jon Hershfield, writes with a deep compassion for all who suffer from Harm OCD, but too often won't seek the help they need due to unwarranted feelings of shame. In this easily readable, inspiring, and informative book, he expertly explains why the best way to deal with Harm OCD is to lean into it and learn how to live with uncertainty. I'm putting it on my 'highly recommended' list."

—**Jonathan Hoffman, PhD, ABPP**, licensed psychologist, cofounder and clinical director of the Neurobehavioral Institute and NBI Ranch in Southeast Florida, member of the Scientific and Clinical Advisory Board of the International OCD Foundation (IOCDF), and author of *Stuck*

"Whether you battle violent obsessions as a sufferer or treatment provider, Jon Hershfield's *Overcoming Harm OCD* will prove to be a potent weapon in your arsenal. As one of the nation's most respected OCD psychotherapists and authors, Jon offers his wisdom and wit in a wonderfully organized and enjoyable-to-read format. His masterful integration of components of cognitive therapy, exposure and response prevention (ERP), acceptance and mindfulness, and self-compassion provide the reader with very practical and effective ways to deflate the debilitating distress that OCD delivers."

—**Charles Brady, PhD, ABPP,** director of the OCD and anxiety program at the Lindner Center of HOPE; vice president at OCD Midwest; associate professor in the department of psychiatry and behavioral neuroscience at the University of Cincinnati College of Medicine

"*Overcoming Harm OCD* breaks down the complexity of Harm OCD into easy-to-understand and practical language. Jon Hershfield's masterful description of unwanted violent obsessions will be greatly appreciated by those affected by these symptoms. His step-by-step instructions and helpful road map for incorporating acceptance and self-compassion are sure to encourage, strengthen, and enhance CBT treatment. This is a must-have resource for clients and professionals alike!"

—**Amy Jacobsen, PhD,** licensed psychologist specializing in the treatment of OCD in Kansas, and coauthor of *Childhood Anxiety Disorders*

"You aren't crazy or bad; you are human. Being human means dealing with difficult things, and OCD is a difficult thing, albeit a very difficult thing. Jon's book addresses the concerns you may have around these challenging thoughts of harm; makes you feel a little bit more normal; and focuses on helping you through it using examples, exercises, and questions. All wrapped in the gold-standard science of CBT for OCD, and supported by mindfulness and self-love. Jon addresses the ways one deals with shame, an often-overlooked emotion that holds back recovery. Having interviewed Jon a few times, I can confidently say that he knows his stuff, but more importantly, he cares."

—**Stuart Ralph,** *The OCD Stories*

"If you have OCD and suffer from violent obsessions, this is the book you need! Jon Hershfield understands the depth of how frightening harm obsessions can be and the intricacies involved when seeking reassurance from the uncertainty they provoke. His compassion for OCD sufferers is demonstrated on every page, and his guidance and knowledge about applying well-established treatment components to face specific harm obsessions offers a clear path to reclaiming your life from OCD. Whether you suffer from harm obsessions or treat clients who do, this book will be become your go-to resource!"

> —**Joan Davidson, PhD**, codirector of the San Francisco Bay Area Center for Cognitive Therapy; assistant professor in the clinical science program at University of California, Berkeley; and author of *Daring to Challenge OCD*

"Hershfield has done it! Using straight-up honesty, compassion, and appropriately placed humor, he has written a body of work tackling the 'untouchable' subject of harm obsessions in OCD. I predict that this book becomes the go-to reference for current and future generations of OCD sufferers, their loved ones, and treating clinicians. Hershfield has deftly avoided being drawn into providing excessive reassurance, which OCD would surely love! Rather, he gifts the reader with tools to live with the uncertainty that we must all face as human beings—specifically with respect to our past and future actions."

> —**S. Evelyn Stewart, MD**, associate professor in the department of psychiatry at the University of British Columbia and director of the Provincial OCD Program at the BC Children's Hospital

"If you have Harm OCD, reading this book will be life-changing. No more thinking you're 'going crazy.' No more avoiding the life you used to love. No more thinking your thoughts aren't normal, because they—and you—are. In *Overcoming Harm OCD*, Jon compassionately demonstrates the H.E.A.Ling power of standing up to your OCD so you can build the full and meaningful life you deserve."

—**Shala Nicely, LPC**, author of *Is Fred in the Refrigerator? Taming OCD and Reclaiming My Life* and cofounder, Beyond the Doubt

"Jon Hershfield has created a masterful, reader-friendly guide to helping individuals with Harm OCD by utilizing step-by-step tools and evidence-based treatment methods. Because this form of OCD is less commonly discussed, I'm glad there is finally a book that provides an in-depth look into the thoughts and experiences of individuals with Harm OCD. This book is a must-read for anyone struggling with unwanted, intrusive violent obsessions, and should be a required read for all clinicians treating clients with Harm OCD."

—**Tabasom Vahidi, PhD**, private practice, works for the Westwood Institute for Anxiety Disorders, Inc.

"Harm OCD is a powerful demon that makes people question their sanity and integrity as a person. Jon eloquently reminds those struggling with this form of OCD that they are not crazy and that self-compassion is important. Through evidence-based strategies, Jon breaks down how to overcome this disabling fear, learn to accept doubt and uncertainty, and live life to its fullest potential. This book is sure to bring hope and relief to those suffering by offering a guided, succinct, easy-to-understand process to overcome their worst fears."

—**Robin Zasio, PsyD, LCSW**, director at The Anxiety Treatment Center of Sacramento, Roseville, and El Dorado Hills; and author of *The Hoarder in You*

"With kind and compassionate humor, Jon Hershfield accomplishes the brilliant task of making a very difficult topic approachable and manageable. Thank you, Jon, for gifting the OCD and mental health communities with your incredible knowledge and insight."

—**Kimberley Quinlan, LMFT**, owner of www.cbtschool.com (providing research-based online courses for OCD, body-focused repetitive behavior (BFRB), and anxiety), and host of the *Your Anxiety Toolkit* podcast

"Jon Hershfield has a gift for writing as if speaking to friends; I know this, as I'm privileged to call Jon a friend, and the wisdom he shares in these pages is imparted with all the warmth, clarity, and compassion that Jon has shown in every conversation we've ever had. By using his extraordinary communication skills to address Harm OCD, Jon offers readers the rare opportunity to learn about this especially difficult mental health challenge from a truly caring and trustworthy friend."

—**Jeff Bell**, author of *Rewind, Replay, Repeat: A Memoir of OCD*

"No matter how it manifests, OCD is painful and disruptive, but Harm OCD tends to add another layer of guilt and shame to the mix. In *Overcoming Harm OCD*, Jon Hershfield recommends love and self-compassion as highly as the gold-standard, evidence-based treatments of the disorder. Using his own H.E.A.L. method to tackle the four main types of harm obsessions, Hershfield walks through common obsessions, compulsions, and example scripts. A resource readers can turn to again and again, *Overcoming Harm OCD* will empower readers to seek help and open up to loved ones."

—**Alison Dotson**, author of *Being Me with OCD*

Overcoming
Harm
OCD

Mindfulness and CBT Tools

for Coping with

Unwanted Violent Thoughts

JON HERSHFIELD, MFT

New Harbinger Publications, Inc.

Publisher's Note

This publication is designed to provide accurate and authoritative information in regard to the subject matter covered. It is sold with the understanding that the publisher is not engaged in rendering psychological, financial, legal, or other professional services. If expert assistance or counseling is needed, the services of a competent professional should be sought.

This is a self-help book and not a clinical manual. It should not be used for self-diagnosis and should not replace the advice of a mental health professional.

Distributed in Canada by Raincoast Books

Copyright © 2018 by Jon Hershfield

New Harbinger Publications, Inc.
5674 Shattuck Avenue
Oakland, CA 94609
www.newharbinger.com

The section "Unhelpful Ideas About Uncertainty Acceptance" is adapted from the author's blog post, "Four Mistaken Beliefs About OCD," for http://www.intrusivethoughts.org. Used by permission.

Cover design by Amy Shoup

Acquired by Jess O'Brien

Edited by Ken Knabb

All Rights Reserved

FSC
www.fsc.org
MIX
Paper from
responsible sources
FSC® C011935

Library of Congress Cataloging-in-Publication Data on file

Printed in the United States of America

23   22

10   9   8   7   6   5   4   3

"Into whatsoever houses I enter, I will enter to help the sick, and I will abstain from all intentional wrongdoing and harm, especially from abusing the bodies of man or woman, bond or free."

—Hippocrates (fifth century BCE)

Contents

Foreword

As Jon mentions in his acknowledgments, I don't write forewords—but here I am. This fact says a great deal about Jon, what I know about him, and why this book is an important addition to OCD therapy. I remember my first meeting with Jon as he was just beginning his rise in the field. We were at a dinner of our peers, all OCD therapists, and the dinner was coming to an end. This was his chance to make an impression. He was sitting across the table from me and caught my eye. Wordlessly, he took the last piece of pizza, licked it, and offered it to me. Never one to turn down a challenge, I took a bite, contaminated it with something worse, and handed it back to him. The contamination challenges escalated, ending with shoes on top of the final remains of the pizza, and, of course, we ate it all. Jon had read the situation, recognized what he had to do, and then boldly and bravely executed his plan, resulting in the outcome he had hoped for. Clearly Jon Hershfield was destined for greatness.

Obsessions about harming are among the most difficult for sufferers to bear. Unlike contamination fears or checking rituals, sharing obsessions about harming is difficult—people outside the OCD community may misunderstand you and believe that you really are at great risk of "snapping" and acting out your fears. In *Overcoming Harm OCD*, Jon provides a place for you to finally understand what is happening to you. And like the night I first met him, when he assessed his audience and knew exactly what to do, Jon not only understands Harm OCD, he is able to explain what is happening to you, why it is happening, and what you need to do. You will find the experience of reading this book more like having a conversation with someone whose expertise and gentle humor make complicated concepts accessible and understandable.

The first two chapters of the book will help you to understand the nature of Harm OCD and the core techniques you will utilize in your treatment. Jon's HEAL acronym for remembering the four cornerstone components of your treatment (cognitive techniques, exposure and response prevention, acceptance and mindfulness, and self-compassion—you will have to read the book to see how he turns this into the HEAL acronym) is only one example of how he makes difficult concepts seem crystal clear.

Armed with the knowledge from those first two chapters, Jon then focuses on the different manifestations of Harm OCD and provides you with examples of the kinds of obsessions and compulsions you are likely to have and details about what you need to do for each of them. What I found most useful in these chapters is the fact that everything made logical sense. I always tell my clients that I don't want them to do anything that I tell them to do unless it makes sense. This book doesn't offer any magic solutions, but it does offer the next best thing: clear, definable steps that you can follow. Although it may not be easy, following these steps will free you from the confines of OCD.

Equally important to describing how to regain control of your life is Jon's explanation of what recovery from OCD looks like. It is not stopping the thoughts that you don't like having; it is learning to be able to think *anything* and to cope with the resulting uncertainty. The way in which you differ from others is not the content of your thoughts. The difference between you and nonsufferers is your obsessive attempts to be 100% certain as to what those thoughts might mean (for example, *Am I bad? Am I more likely to do* x?). Jon's book shows you how you can live with uncertainty.

In summary, I urge you to listen to Jon and to learn from his understanding of OCD and his ability to translate that understanding into a clear treatment plan for successfully managing and coping with your OCD. And I hope that you, like Jon at that dinner where I first met him, will boldly and bravely execute that plan and start your journey to freedom.

—Jonathan Grayson
The Grayson LA Treatment Center for Anxiety and OCD
Pasadena, California

Introduction

You're going to be okay. Before I say anything else, let me say this. You're going to be okay. You are not crazy. You are not a horrible person. If this book makes any sense to you at all, then you will come to understand how a glitch in your mind is making you *think* you're a monster. But you are not a monster. You're going to get on top of this.

This is a book about overcoming Harm OCD (or aggressive obsessions), a form of obsessive-compulsive disorder (OCD) that manifests primarily as intrusive thoughts about behaving in a way that would purposefully or unintentionally cause harm to oneself or others (Moulding, Aardema, and O'Connor 2014). There are four well-understood dimensions of OCD, known as harm, unacceptable thoughts, contamination, and symmetry (Abramowitz et al. 2010). These are not four different disorders, but four ways in which unwanted thoughts and compulsive responses manifest in OCD. This book sets out to organize what we understand about OCD when it manifests in this particular dimension. It also offers a series of strategies that work for any kind of OCD, but allows the reader to tailor it specifically to Harm OCD.

When I was first learning to stand up to my own OCD, I found a great deal of solace in taking part in online support groups. It was there that I read the stories of thousands of other brave OCD sufferers. Some of these people shared my particular obsessions, some of them didn't, but most of them seemed to think the same *way* I did. Many of them identified as having "Harm" OCD. I don't personally identify as having Harm OCD, but I have always experienced some kind of steady stream of unsolicited mental junkmail, often involving violent or repugnant thoughts. I noticed in those online forums that I had many of the same unwanted thoughts as Harm OCD sufferers, *except that I was not worried that those thoughts would be acted on.* On the contrary, when I was around thirteen and discovered horror movies, I felt *comforted* by what I saw. Someone else was picking up this signal in his head too! The first time I saw the film *Hellraiser*, in which characters are routinely stripped of their skin with hooks attached to chains by deformed monsters whose clothes are sewn into their own flesh, it produced in me a bizarre sense of peace. When I saw the film's iconic monster, an articulate demon with nails hammered all over his face in a perfectly symmetrical grid pattern, I thought: Now *there's* a guy who knows about staying calm under pressure and living *with* the unwanted!

I think my decision early on to go ahead and just *have* the violent thoughts, instead of trying to block them out, inoculated me from allowing this type of OCD to fully take shape. I required therapy only for the thoughts I *refused* to accept. I think I barely missed having Harm OCD because I decided early on that my intrusive violent thoughts weren't going anywhere; that I could live with them and that I didn't have to worry about them becoming actions or keeping me from living a joyful life. These are lessons that I hope you, too, can learn from this book.

There May Be Triggers Ahead

In this book, I will be talking about violent obsessions, and this means I will be using some potentially upsetting words to describe how violent obsessions are experienced. I will also be giving examples of ways to expose oneself to the fear of violent thoughts, and this necessarily means using violent words. I may mention the name of a weapon that triggers your unwanted thoughts. I may describe a narrative about a person being harmed in a violent way, which may trigger your unwanted thoughts. I will not pull any punches (pun intended?) and may speak frankly, bluntly, or at times even brutally or obscenely. I will try to do what OCD refuses to do and couch my abrasive language in a helpful context, but nonetheless, you may find some of the material in this book discomforting.

Though this book cannot function as a replacement for treatment, I hope it can shine some light on your symptoms and your well-deserved hope for getting past them.

About This Book

Typically, I would recommend reading an OCD book cover-to-cover even if there are chapters that don't seem to apply to you. There is a lot to be learned about one form of OCD by understanding other forms of it. However, given how focused on a specific theme this book is, it could be equally effective if you read through the first two chapters (on assessment, understanding violent thoughts, and treatment tools) and then jump to the chapter you think most applies to you after that. Some readers may be concerned that reading about different ways Harm OCD manifests could result in more material for the OCD to attach to. If this is your concern, that's quite all right. My hope is that by the end of the book, you will have a better understanding of your mind and its relationship to Harm OCD and that you will intuitively grasp that you don't need to be afraid of new thoughts. They are, after all, just other thoughts. Perhaps you will later return to the rest of the book out of curiosity about your fellow Harm OCD sufferers.

Part 1 of this book is a primer on Harm OCD, how it is assessed and how it can be treated. In chapter 1, I go over what Harm OCD is, some theories as to why we have violent thoughts, and how clinicians assess for OCD and distinguish violent obsessions in this disorder from other kinds of relationships people have to their violent thoughts. In chapter 2, I discuss the role of uncertainty acceptance in mastering your Harm OCD and four treatment tools to get you there: cognitive approaches, exposure and response prevention, mindfulness, and self-compassion.

Part 2 of this book separates Harm OCD into focused subthemes and takes the tools described in part 1 and applies them to each of these in detail. As mentioned above, you may want to jump to your subtheme on the first reading if you feel nervous about exposing yourself to other variations of Harm OCD you haven't already come across. Chapter 3 explores the fear of having or developing a harmful identity, including the fear of intending harm and of causing harm through a failure of responsibility. Chapter 4 discusses unwanted intrusive thoughts about impulsively harming others through violence. Chapter 5 focuses on unwanted thoughts of self-harm. Chapter 6 addresses Harm OCD that specifically focuses on harming one's children.

Part 3 is about the next steps. Chapter 7 discusses how to access appropriate treatment for your Harm OCD, understanding Harm OCD in children, and disclosing your condition to your loved ones and others in ways that allow them to be an effective part of your support network. Chapter 8 brings our journey to a close with a discussion of the role of shame in Harm OCD and ways to achieve long-term mastery over your obsessions.

Who Are the Harm OCD Sufferers?

I'm going to introduce you to four fictional people, composites of people I've encountered in my clinical work and in the process of my contributions to online support groups. Each of these characters represents a version of what I will be referring to as Harm OCD throughout this book.

Joanna

Joanna put the roach traps exactly where the exterminator said they should go, well out of reach of the children and pets. Then she took out the trash, and then washed her hands. An hour later, the thought popped into her head that her husband usually takes out the trash. Then it occurred to her that she had taken out the trash with hands that had touched the roach traps and could potentially have had poison on them. Did she know this when she touched the trash cans? Did she intentionally leave poison on the trash cans for her husband to later touch? Should she warn him? Does this indicate that somewhere deep in her subconscious she is some kind of closeted sociopath who doesn't care if her husband lives or dies? Why did she allow potential harm to come someone's way? Is she a bad person? Then the confessing started…Every day, multiple times a day, her husband had to be on the receiving end of detailed descriptions of what she touched, what she thought, and when. He had to respond that he understood and that he didn't believe she was a dangerous person, but she would never be completely satisfied by his answers, and the confessions and questions persisted.

I'll explore Joanna's challenges in more detail in chapter 3. To your friends and family, you may be thought of as a worrywart, or maybe even a pessimist or cynic. But you know that your concerns run much deeper than the outside world can appreciate. For you, it's a battle for your humanity, a battle of good versus evil wherein your side of the battle gets determined only at the end. But developing mastery over your OCD reveals a much more joyful life ahead.

Mandy

Mandy remembers exactly where she was sitting when she saw the news about Marjory Stoneman Douglas High School. A young man had walked into the school and begun shooting, killing seventeen children and wounding several others. Mandy asked her husband, "Why would someone do that?" He just shrugged, an unsatisfying answer. How could someone do that? Something in her made her want to check the news again, collect more information. Why did she even want to collect more information? The more she thought about it, the more she found herself asking, How do I know I wouldn't do that? Why can't I control these thoughts? Then the nightmare began…Everything that had anything to do with violence became completely overwhelming. The TV couldn't be trusted, even books at school that mentioned violent acts led to tearful nights of tossing and turning. Sharp objects or weapons of any kind had to be avoided or they would come with thoughts of mentally "snapping" and lunging maniacally at people in a fit of bloodlust. She was pretty sure the other day when she saw her husband cutting a tomato that she felt something in her hand like she was about to grab the knife from him and plunge it into his throat. She kept telling herself she would never do it and then she'd start having thoughts like, You could have done it, you might do it, better stay away just in case. Even places where violent things might have happened couldn't be visited in case they reminded her of her feared secret self.

If you relate to Mandy's story, you may feel that life is like walking a never-ending tightrope on a windy day. I'll cover Mandy's assets and liabilities in the fight against OCD in chapter 4. You're not an abomination because of these thoughts. You have a particular sensitivity to these naturally occurring mental events and you're here right now learning to address it.

Elizabeth

Elizabeth was not suicidal. She was not even depressed. Sure, she got low moods from time to time, and even joked about how she'd rather die than go to work tomorrow for that meeting. One day she was looking out her office window on the fourth floor and the thought occurred, What if I jumped? At first it didn't bother her at all, just one of those silly thoughts she gets sometimes. But then, on her drive home, the thought popped into her head, What if I just turned my car into the oncoming traffic? She turned the radio on to distract herself. Nirvana. Didn't the lead singer of Nirvana kill himself? One by one, everything seemed to lead her to think about killing or maiming herself for no reason. She started to wonder if these were signs, not coincidences, and what if she had some underlying motive to commit suicide? She took all the knives and hid them away. Better take all the pills in the house and get rid of them too, she thought. No more driving, too scary. What about bleach? She could drink bleach! Better get rid of it, she thought. She loved her life, but now it didn't matter how much she reassured herself, something in her mind seemed to be trying to kill her!

But it doesn't have to all fall apart from there. OCD seems to strip you of all the things that make you free, one at a time, making your existence narrower and narrower until you beg for mercy. But there's nothing crazy about wanting to feel confident in your faculties, wanting to feel safe in your own skin and safe from leaving your loved ones behind. The question is, how can you access that confidence without just surviving from compulsion to compulsion? Becoming a student of your Harm OCD can put you back in command of your life. I'll explore Elizabeth's brand of Harm OCD in chapter 5.

Richard

Richard was so proud of being a dad. His infant son had just started to make eye contact with him. One day, for no apparent reason, the thought popped into his head, I could shoot my son. Richard hated guns, why would he even think of that? Suddenly it seemed that guns were everywhere. Sporting goods stores sell them, gun shows come to town, his neighbor goes hunting...he could get the gun from the neighbor! Could he do it? Why? Why would he even want to know this? He loves his son, doesn't he? Doesn't he??? Grotesque images of his sweet, innocent baby's shattered brains inside the crib flooded his mind nearly every waking moment. Even sleep provided no respite, as he would simply dream of guns and blood all night. His wife became frustrated with him as he would always find ways to avoid being alone with his son and rarely volunteered to help with diaper changes or bathing. But how could he take the risk of being a dad if it meant risking his son's life?

Loving someone as much as you love your child can be a magnet for Harm OCD. The worst thing you can imagine is being responsible for causing your child pain or death. If you relate to Richard's story, it may seem incredibly unfair that the universe puts this helpless creature in your hands and also gives you a mind that seems to delight in challenging your competence as a parent. The tips and tools discussed in chapter 6 can help you liberate yourself from OCD's trickery.

The four brave souls above represent the four forms of violent obsessions I will be discussing in this book—fear of having a harmful identity, fear of acting out harmfully to others, fear of self-harming, and fear of harming one's children. They do not capture every specific way Harm OCD manifests, and it is not unusual to have elements of each of these examples co-occurring. Your OCD may be telling you right now that you don't fit perfectly into any of the above stories and that this must mean something dreadful about you. Try to reserve judgment against yourself and let the OCD go ahead and read the book alongside you. Try to respond to its incessant negative commentary the way my wife responds to my wisecracks when we watch romantic comedies (she ignores me, I think).

PART 1

Understanding Harm OCD

I n this section of the book, I will discuss some OCD basics, and more specifically, what Harm OCD is and what it is not. I will also explore the nature of violent thoughts and the role uncertainty acceptance plays in OCD. Lastly, I will identify some of the main tools and techniques that are effective for OCD treatment. There's a lot of information coming your way, and don't be surprised when your OCD tells you it's too much to handle. Also, get ready for incoming thoughts about not having OCD in the first place! OCD wants you to view this book as a "get out of harm free" card. Anything you read that doesn't fit perfectly with your worries will get used by the OCD as evidence that your fears will come true. It's okay to pace yourself. Read this book slowly if it's overwhelming right now. It's also okay to let those thoughts come and go.

CHAPTER 1

Defining Harm OCD

What do we mean when we say "Harm OCD"? How is it assessed and diagnosed? Right, all you want to know right now is whether or not you are going to hurt someone (or yourself). But bear with me. The answer to this question will be more impactful when you understand more about OCD overall. In my clinical experience, OCD sufferers often start off on the wrong foot, presuming that their thoughts are irrational madness. This is not technically true, at least not in the way you are likely to see it. There's nothing irrational, or even unusual, about wanting to keep yourself and others safe, about wanting to be a morally responsible person, or about wanting to be confident that you'll be able to experience and share joy without your mind ruining every moment. These are reasonable things to desire. Where things get distorted, or *disordered*, is when we seek certainty about our fears and try too hard to guarantee that they won't come true.

Understanding Violent Obsessions in OCD

OCD is a common mental health challenge characterized by unwanted intrusive thoughts that are upsetting as well as by compulsions, which are behaviors aimed at reducing this distress (American Psychiatric Association [APA] 2013). Approximately 2.3% of adults experience clinically diagnosable OCD at some point in their life (Ruscio et al. 2010). According to the APA's *Diagnostic and Statistical Manual V*

(*DSM-V*), obsessions and compulsions must be time-consuming and/ or cause distress or impairment, and they can't be attributed to some other mental disorder or medical condition (APA 2013).

Obsessions Are...

We usually associate the word "obsession" with thoughts only, but the *DSM-V* also includes *images* and *urges* in this category (APA 2013). Since we tend to think of our obsessions as unwanted thoughts, but think of urges as synonymous with desires, the language can be scary and confusing. Understanding the meaning of each term in the context of OCD can help.

Thoughts: The problem with defining the word "thought" is that every definition we have of "thought" is just a synonym for the word. We use words like idea, opinion, notion, and so on. A thought is a mental event of *some* kind and the problem with such a loose and abstract definition is that it provides us with little information about how seriously we are supposed to take our thoughts. Let's agree that a thought is a *mental event* that you become aware of. A good way to conceptualize it is the internal experience put into language. For example, I may have a memory of eating eggs for breakfast and the thought is "I had eggs for breakfast." Or the thought may present as a question, as in, "What did I have for breakfast?" Or the thought could present as an idea, such as, "I should have eggs for breakfast." The intrinsic value of any thought is unknown. It is simply made up of words, like you might come across in a book. When we identify these mental events as unwanted or intrusive, and repetitive, we call them obsessions.

Images: While many thoughts come in the form of language, it is also common to experience thoughts as images or pictures in the mind. In OCD, these images may come suddenly, like a flash of a still-frame image projected onto the screen of the mind, or they may come repeatedly, like scenes of a scary movie unfolding in your head. Though these images are not literally being seen with the eyes (as in a visual hallucination), the vivid imagination of an OCD sufferer can make the experience plenty upsetting. Problems arise when we try to get certainty about why the images are there; whether they'll ever go away (and stay away); and whether they may represent predictions, memories, or desires.

Urges: The word "urge" is generally defined as a strong desire. This is a good example of where a word means something different in an OCD context than elsewhere. Just as someone may say they have a "chocolate obsession" or a "*Star Wars* obsession" and this does not mean they have debilitating unwanted thoughts about these things, we use the word "urge" to describe something differently in an OCD context than more generally. I might say I have an urge to eat when I'm watching a movie and smell popcorn, but it is completely acceptable for me to have this experience. People with Harm OCD often describe their intrusive thoughts as "urges" because it's difficult to find another word for the marriage of an intrusive thought and a sensation in the body that seems to indicate an imminent action. If you feel like your hand wants to move near a knife, you may interpret that as a scary *urge* to grab the knife and use it for harm. But this is actually better understood in OCD as a *feeling* obsession, or an intrusive feeling, not a genuine urge. You may believe that you must perfectly distinguish between a thought and an urge, but as you continue with this book, you will come to understand that this certainty-seeking behavior is a trap.

Compulsions Are...

A compulsion can be understood as any mental or physical attempt to suppress or neutralize obsessions. They are typically repetitive (they have to be because they don't work!) and they stem from a drive to get certainty about your imagined threats. Sometimes they may appear to only be focused on reducing anxiety, but usually that anxiety reduction is connected to the belief that the behavior has proven the OCD wrong. In other words, OCD says something scary and your compulsive behavior (including mental behavior) says, "No way! Can't be!" A compulsion in Harm OCD is anything you do, mentally or otherwise, to try to convince yourself that you *did not, will not, would not,* and *are not harming people.* A compulsion is viewed as a prerequisite for shifting your attention on to the next task. The specific actions (and mental behaviors) may vary from case to case, which we will explore further in part 2 of this book. But here's a general list of compulsions you might experience in Harm OCD:

- avoiding things, activities, or people that trigger thoughts of harm

- engaging in safety behaviors (for example, hiding objects that could be weapons)

- checking to make sure you haven't harmed or wouldn't harm yourself or anyone else

- mentally reviewing memories or hypothetical scenarios to assure yourself that no harm could have been done or can be done

- engaging in superstitious behaviors to ensure that no harm will take place

- confessing unwanted harm thoughts

- seeking reassurance from others that harm-related thoughts are acceptable or that harmful acts did not or would not take place

- repeatedly researching the difference between OCD and a propensity to cause harm

The Obsessive-Compulsive Cycle

No book on OCD is complete without a picture and explanation of the obsessive-compulsive cycle. The graphic below demonstrates the flow of obsessions to compulsions and back again. A person first experiences an obsession, which then results in distress (such as anxiety, disgust, or some other kind of discomfort). Next, the person attempts to reduce that distress by engaging in a compulsion. For example, you might get an intrusive thought about harming someone and then reduce anxiety about this thought by repeating the phrase "I would never harm someone" until you feel better. The problem is, the moment you feel better, you trigger a process in the brain called *negative reinforcement*. Everything we do, we do because it has either been reinforced or not reinforced. If you go to work, you get paid, and this payment is enjoyed and sends the message to the brain, "Hey, you should go to work again tomorrow." This is called positive reinforcement. You then wake up the next day with an urge to go get paid. Obsessions are reinforced by the removal of an unwanted experience (distress), so this process is referred to as *negative* reinforcement. The more relief compulsions bring, the more the brain attaches compulsive urges to unwanted thoughts. So the more you try to reassure yourself about an unwanted violent thought, the more the brain pushes you to make sure you respond this way every time you have a violent thought.

The Obsessive-Compulsive Cycle

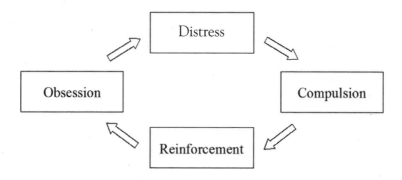

Who Has Harm OCD?

In this book, I will use the term "Harm OCD" to describe any manifestation of OCD where the obsessive theme centers around violent
content, though there may be other ways in which you worry about
causing harm (this will be discussed in chapter 3). Our understanding
of how many people struggle with violent obsessions is still developing.
One study suggested that 28% of people with OCD report violent
obsessions (Rasmussen and Eisen 1992). Another suggested that up to
50% of people with OCD have violent obsessions (Rasmussen and
Tsuang 1986). Further, as many as 70% of youth with OCD report
having aggressive obsessions (Storch et al. 2007).

Suffice it to say, violent obsessions in OCD are not some fringe
symptom, so why do we hear so little about them? One reason likely
has to do with the nature of the disorder itself. While the majority of
the population has unwanted and intrusive thoughts, people with
OCD are likely to attach special meaning to them, rather than just
assuming they are the spam email of the mind. This leads to a lot of
shame and self-stigma, as well as concerns about being misunderstood
by others. In fact, shame has been found to be particularly high in
those with Harm OCD (Wetterneck, Singh, and Hart 2014). Another
reason Harm OCD gets so little attention is that its sufferers may be
less easily portrayed in the media than those with obvious physical
compulsions (such as excessive washing or checking), so people are not
used to "seeing" it.

People with Harm OCD often consider themselves part of the
"pure o" community. What this means is they may see themselves as
having obsessions, but not responding to them by engaging in compulsions. The DSM-V's first criterion for OCD is the presence of obsessions, compulsions, *or* both, but studies show that people with OCD all
experience obsessions *and* compulsions (Leonard and Riemann 2012).
This confusion may have to do with a misconception that physical
compulsions, such as excessive handwashing, are the only kind of
compulsions. As referenced above, the *DSM-V* also includes "mental
acts" as part of the definition of compulsions. In fact, mental compulsions and reassurance seeking are compulsions often associated with

these types of obsessions (Williams et al. 2011). You may have some resistance to the idea that there's nothing special about your experience with Harm OCD that sets it aside from other forms of OCD. Harm-related obsessions can be so torturous that sometimes even acknowledging that you play a role in them by doing mental rituals and other compulsions may seem too painful. Further, having intrusive thoughts that reflect cultural taboos is inherently isolating. It can thus be useful to connect with others who feel that their obsessions are forbidden (as opposed to obsessions with more culturally accepted themes, such as concern about germs or doubt about having locked the door), and this is often done in online communities under the unfortunately misleading heading "pure o." Having a community-building name of any kind can be helpful for reducing the sense of isolation, but it is important to understand that the types of mental acts people with Harm OCD engage in are no less identifiable, compulsive, or *treatable* than more overt physical rituals.

Why Do We Have Violent Thoughts?

The first thing to remember is that human beings have violent thoughts because that is a normal thought process to have. This is worth repeating—having violent thoughts is normal. For most of human existence, our survival has depended on violence. Today, as we live in more tightly connected communities with more advanced forms of communicating our needs and desires with one another, we rely somewhat less on violence to get by. Though you wouldn't know it from watching the news (which we easily forget presents us mostly with unusual occurrences, which is what makes it news!), violence has rather steadily declined over the last few thousand years. We may actually be living in the most peaceful time for humanity ever. But it hasn't always been this way. We come from violent pasts as a species, from beating each other with clubs over a carcass to settling an argument with a duel outside the saloon. (See Steven Pinker's *The Better Angels of Our Nature* [2011] for an exploration of this topic.) So violence in the mind may simply be a relic inherited from our ancestors.

Lee Baer, in his seminal book on "bad" thoughts, *Imp of the Mind*, discusses three perspectives on violent thoughts (Baer 2001, 45-51):

- Evolutionary theories: that violent thoughts may be an inherited survival mechanism of old. In other words, we have violence on the mind because violence has historically been necessary to us as a species.

- Freudian theory: that violent thoughts arise from conflict between desire and the constraints of society. Freud believed that mental health conditions arose due to our frustration between the sexual urges we have at different theoretical stages of development and our inability to express them in a world of laws and social norms.

- The problem of thought suppression: that we make thoughts intrusive by trying to suppress them. Daniel Wegner's excellent book *White Bears and Other Unwanted Thoughts* (1989) explains the results of research that shows how efforts to keep thoughts from occurring actually cause them to increase in your awareness.

You Notice and You Worry That You Noticed

Another way to look at this is that our brains are adept at running potentials. In other words, they are always calculating whether violence, sex, food, or anything else might be occurring. Concepts like sex and food don't always request our attention at convenient times, either. People with OCD may just be more likely to notice all of these potentials and attribute meaning to the noticing.

Imagine that all thoughts are available to be had at any time, as if they are just lying there waiting to be noticed. When you say you are "having" a thought, you mean that your mind is specifically attending to that thought's presence. People with OCD may be attending to a wider variety of thoughts at any give time and then confusing this problem of attention with the importance of the individual thought.

(See *The Mindfulness Workbook for OCD* by Hershfield and Corboy [2013] for further exploration of this concept.)

One study found that people who fear losing control are more likely to become aware of and upset by intrusive aggressive thoughts when provoked by an imagined situation of having their goals interfered with. In other words, if I have a goal and that goal is thwarted, I feel frustrated and this results in the presence of an aggressive thought. Those without the fear of loss of control are less burdened by the presence of such thoughts, viewing them as, well, silly. The study suggested that intrusive harm thoughts are not always just randomly occurring events, but naturally occurring responses to frustrating situations that people with OCD are overresponding to (Riskind, Ayers, and Wright 2007).

Why They Are So Persistent

Even if you can get behind the notion that these thoughts pop up for acceptable reasons, you may still be worried about the fact that they seem so relentless. Why do they keep coming at you? Cognitive models of OCD credit a tendency among those with the disorder to evaluate these thoughts in specifically problematic ways (Purdon 2004):

- Overvalued responsibility—thinking that any potential contribution to harm makes you responsible for all harm that occurs (for example, thinking you are a murderer if someone gets in a car crash because they were distracted by the glare off a gum wrapper in the street you saw but didn't pick up)

- Thought-action fusion—thinking that the quantity of the thought equals the likelihood of it coming true, or thinking that the presence of the thought is morally the same as having acted on it (we will explore this further in chapter 2)

- Thought control—believing that failure to fully control thoughts will lead to failure to control anything (including actions)

Compulsions, as discussed above, reinforce these beliefs, leading to greater thought intrusion, more of these mistaken appraisals, more compulsions, and so on.

Thinking Violence Is Not Being Violent

The key thing to remember in all of these explanations is that none of them point to anything actually being wrong with *you*, except maybe some tactical errors in your approach. Violent thoughts are events that occur in the mind, not bad choices you are making with bad intentions. Understanding that we do not control what thoughts we are aware of in any given moment allows us to view thoughts with more freedom and less judgment. Since we can't pick and choose our thoughts, we are allowed to observe them in different ways without self-blame. In other words, we are not required to actually hate all violent thoughts in order to be nonviolent, moral people.

Consider that violent thoughts can even be exciting and enjoyable for some, such as the thrill of blowing something up in a video game. Violent thoughts can also be funny or absurd, such as the scene in the movie *Airplane!* where passengers line up to use increasingly unhelpful acts of violence to try to calm a woman having a panic attack on a plane. Violent thoughts can be creative, such as movie monsters with different powers to capture their victims in unusual ways. For example, in *A Nightmare on Elm Street*, Freddy Krueger is burned to death by the townsfolk for being a child killer and executes his revenge by haunting the dreams of the town's teenagers, using their personal fears as weapons of execution. Violent thoughts can even be inspirational, as in expressions of patriotism celebrating the violent overthrow of oppressors (for example, "And the rockets' red glare, the bombs bursting in air" in "The Star Spangled Banner"). Having violent thoughts, unwanted *or otherwise*, is not an automatic human failure. It is an automatic human experience, and our feelings about violence can vary wildly.

People with OCD are probably less likely to commit acts of violence than anyone else. Considering how prevalent OCD is and the high rate of violent obsessions within the OCD population, it's worth pointing out that "there are virtually no reports in the literature of patients with OCD who act violently," and that having obsessions and OCD may even in fact be protective against violent actions (Booth et al. 2014). Knowing this won't keep your OCD from accusing you of being the outlier or making you dwell on the word "virtually" in the last sentence, but it's okay to let this knowledge boost your confidence and willingness to get treated.

Assessing for Harm OCD

OCD can usually be diagnosed with a simple clinical interview by a therapist who understands obsessions and compulsions and how to identify them. This may include using a checklist or "scale" that asks about common obsessions and compulsions, such as the Yale Brown Obsessive Compulsive Scale (the YBOCS, or the child version known as CYBOCS) (Goodman et al. 1989; Scahill et al. 1997). Do you have unwanted intrusive thoughts that cause you distress? Do you respond to them with time-consuming rituals and avoidance? Does this impair your quality of life in a meaningful way? Then you probably have OCD.

Assessing Harm OCD is no different from assessing other forms of OCD. The standard YBOCS-II asks about these "aggressive obsessions" and compulsive behaviors:

Fear might harm self or others because not careful enough. Examples: parked car rolling down hill, hit a pedestrian because not paying attention, customer gets injured because you gave him wrong materials or information.

Fear might harm self on impulse.* Examples: impulsively swallowing poison, driving car into oncoming traffic, cutting self with nearby knife.

*Distinguish from suicidal intent.

Fear might harm others on impulse.* Examples: physically harming loved ones, stabbing or poisoning dinner guests, driving car into oncoming traffic, pushing stranger in front of a train.

*Distinguish from homicidal intent.

Violent, horrific, or repulsive images. Examples: intrusive and disturbing images of car crashes or disfigured people.*

*Distinguish from PTSD.

Checking that nothing terrible did or will happen. In Harm OCD, this may include checking to see if someone has any cuts or bruises that you might have caused somehow, checking the news for evidence of a feared act, or checking to see if you would commit a violent act or have access to a weapon.

Need to tell, ask, or confess things. Many people with Harm OCD avoid talking about their unwanted thoughts for fear of being judged negatively. But many also repeatedly tell people about their violent thoughts to get certainty that the other person is informed of any imagined danger or to reduce guilt about having the thoughts in secret.

Mental rituals (other than checking or counting). Some may repeat prayers or other statements to neutralize unwanted thoughts. Other mental rituals may include thought exercises such as running through scenarios where harm is possible and testing to see how they would feel or analyzing whether the scenarios could come true. Mentally reviewing past acts to try to get certainty that no harm was done is another common mental ritual.

Avoiding handling sharp or dangerous objects, or operating vehicles or machinery, out of concern might harm others. This may also include avoiding places where harming devices could be found, such as a sporting goods store.

> Avoiding contact with people, children, or animals because of unwanted impulses.
>
> Avoiding watching TV, listening to the radio, or reading the newspaper to shield from disturbing information. This may also include avoiding violent video games or even "aggressive" music that one imagines could produce dangerous feelings.
>
> (Storch et al. 2010a)

The few compulsions listed above may be the ones most likely to be directly associated with Harm OCD. However, OCD is not a neatly distinct disorder and it has a way of working itself into multiple layers of experience. Thus, other common compulsions, such as repeating behaviors or excessively washing hands (also asked about on the YBOCS and other assessment scales), could just as easily be done with the intention to ward off unwanted violent thoughts. Similarly, other obsessions, such as moral or religious fears, can occupy the same mental space as Harm OCD if you believe it to be morally wrong or sinful to have a violent thought. It can be helpful to remember that assessment tools (and the clinicians who administer and analyze them) ask a wide array of questions to form a three-dimensional picture of your OCD. So don't be confused if you identify with one area of OCD and not another, or if you identify with many areas of OCD. This says nothing about your prognosis or severity. It just provides information about how to tailor treatment specifically to you.

The Scary World of Extreme Checking

No, it's not a new sports craze. What I mean by "extreme checking" is when desperation and compulsion collide to cause behaviors that could be potentially harmful despite not including any actual intention to cause harm. For example, a person terribly afraid of harming his infant daughter might gently hold a pillow over the baby's face thinking it would prove he won't try to suffocate her. This is a bad idea on multiple levels. First, and most obviously, it could cause harm by accident. Second, it doesn't prove anything other than that he is afraid of causing harm, which he already knew. The message that he is a danger to his child is actually *enhanced* by efforts to prove that he is not. Consider what happens when you take the bait in any argument. You can't help but concede that there is a debate worth having when you go on the defensive. If I say I have a pet unicorn and you say "Oh really, where do you keep it?" then you give me an opportunity to talk to you about my pet unicorn like it's real. If instead you simply let me make my claim and refuse to dignify it with a counterclaim, I will be left hanging with my own ridiculousness.

Compulsions always prime the pump for stronger obsessions. Extreme checking behaviors have the (very high) potential to become their own triggers once you realize you used someone you care about as a guinea pig in a behavioral experiment and start to obsess over whether or not you went too far. In short, checking is a compulsion and compulsions never work. Extreme checking behaviors create even more problems. If you find yourself engaging in such behaviors, remember that it doesn't mean you are a bad person or that you are more likely to cause harm, but it *does* mean you need to take the severity of your OCD more seriously.

Reassurance Seeking Never Works

Of all of the compulsions you may engage in to try to escape these unwanted thoughts, reassurance seeking may be the most insidious. The first time you ask someone to tell you that you won't act on your thoughts, it may feel like a satisfying rush of relief when they tell you there's no way you'll do it. But this rush doesn't last longer than any other kind of high, and the OCD quickly pokes holes in the reassurance. *How do they know what I will or won't do? What if they don't really understand what I meant when I shared these thoughts? What if they're just telling me what I want to hear? How can they say I won't hurt anyone when they don't know this new thought I just had?* The more you ask, the more aggressive the OCD gets, the more you think you need the reassurance just to feel stable for a moment. Reassurance seeking never works. You get burned either way. You either get the answer you want, which validates and strengthens the OCD, or you don't get the answer you want, which terrifies you and again validates and strengthens the OCD. Bringing the Internet into the equation by googling your thoughts and trying to make your own differential diagnosis makes everything worse.

Differential Diagnosis

Picking up this book with the word "Harm" in the title may have been a scary endeavor. Admitting to yourself that you have unwanted intrusive thoughts of a violent nature is hard enough, but to allow yourself to be seen or heard by others admitting this may take your anxiety to another level. Every act of defiance against OCD is worth celebrating, so give yourself a tip of the hat for getting here.

Obsessive-compulsive disorder is a clever little beast because one of its hallmark traits is to make you question whether or not you have it. The underlying fear is that these unwanted thoughts have some kind of special meaning, either that they are predictive of an unwanted future act or that they say something unacceptable about your identity. So naturally you will want to know that the problem is OCD and not something more nefarious. OCD is not difficult to assess. For starters, we could simply ask if these intrusive thoughts are unwanted and distressing. But the truth about mental health is that people don't always fit nicely into little categories determined by the American Psychiatric Association. People have the criteria for one disorder, but may have other disorders (disturbingly referred to as "co-morbid" disorders) or other influencing factors in their mood, environment, or physical health that impact whether they may have obsessions and compulsions.

To get the proper treatment for OCD, you need to get an accurate diagnosis from a professional trained in treating OCD. Someone with no experience treating OCD may not know what questions to ask that can help you articulate your experience well. This stuff is hard to talk about and if you, the thinker, are confused, then adding a confused clinician to the mix may make things worse. Self-diagnosis, *especially* regarding unwanted harm thoughts, is also particularly unreliable and I would recommend generally avoiding any online "tests" for Harm OCD. The person analyzing the test data (you) may be suffering from OCD and the OCD is biased against you.

What Isn't Harm OCD? a.k.a. the Scariest Few Paragraphs in This Book

As mentioned above, there are many ways that violent thoughts can show up in the mind that are not necessarily OCD. This is a scary thing to consider if your OCD is telling you that you may cause harm. Some people have OCD and that's that. Some people have OCD that is being affected or mediated by something that isn't OCD. Some people have symptoms that may look like OCD but aren't. And some people may have OCD as well as another disorder that is not OCD, or a symptom that is not typically found in OCD. So if Harm OCD means having obsessive thoughts of violence, then what *isn't* Harm OCD?

- **Genuine desire to cause harm:** I know, "How do I know if my thoughts are a genuine desire or not?" Well, the fact that you are so unclear about it points to OCD. People who have a genuine desire to cause harm to self or others may or may not *enjoy* their thoughts about harm, but they view them as lining up well with their preferred or historic identity. This is sometimes referred to as "ego syntonic," which means that the thoughts make sense to the thinkers given the context of how the thinkers view themselves in the world. One of the things that makes your harm thoughts so upsetting is that they are ego *dystonic*, meaning they do not line up well with your preferred or historic identity. *Why would I, of all people, be thinking such horrible things?* This is an OCD sufferer's question. People with antisocial personality disorder, for example, demonstrate a pervasive disregard for the rights of others and this has nothing to do with Harm OCD.

- **People with impulse control disorders and related disorders:** Some people commit acts of harm because they have a problem in the brain that fails to inhibit them from responding to impulses. In Harm OCD, where the concern is about causing harm impulsively, this concept is terrifying. People who have a history of committing brief and random violent acts in response to sudden bursts of aggression are not Harm OCD sufferers. While they may feel badly afterwards, they do not typically have a history of worrying about the behavior prior to the event. The event is unexpected, spontaneous, and unanticipated. Many people with Harm OCD worry about impulses turning into actions and interpret them as warnings that an action is about to occur, but this is best understood as an unwanted, intrusive sensation. In the book *Overcoming Unwanted Intrusive Thoughts*, the authors describe "a whoosh of fear" that coincides with struggling against intrusive thoughts and point out that this often gets confused with impulses. However, people with impulse control disorders "'act first and think later' whereas you are an 'over-thinker'" (Winston and Seif 2017, 16).

- **Personality disorders:** Some mental health challenges are understood as a series of rigid character traits and patterns of behavior, such as instability in relationships, excessive dependence on or avoidance of others, or intermittent bursts of anger. In some cases, people with personality disorders may become so emotionally overheated that they experience urges to engage in violent acts or acts of self-harm (cutting, for example). The thoughts preceding these acts may bring relief, as opposed to the distress typically experienced with an obsessive fear of violent thoughts.

- **Severe depression with suicidality:** If you obsess about thoughts related to suicide, your biggest fear is that you might impulsively choose to end your life. This is fundamentally different from people who genuinely desire not to live because they are so severely depressed and don't want the experience to persist any longer. People with OCD do sometimes struggle with what is called suicidal ideation, which is simply a desire to die. It can be passive (that is, it does not include a plan) or active (that is, it includes a plan and intent). This is different from obsessively fearing self-harm. In major depressive disorders, it is not intrusive suicidal thoughts that cause distress, but the symptoms of low mood, fatigue, and hopelessness that can lead to suicidal ideation. Suicidal thoughts may be viewed favorably as an escape from depression or as a way to stop being the "burden" to others that they imagine themselves being. A trained professional can help assess whether there is a safety concern including intent, means, or a plan for suicide.

- **Bipolar disorder:** Some people suffer from a mood disorder that involves cycles of depressed mood and episodes of "mania." Manic episodes often include periods of impulsivity, insomnia, hyperactivity, and sometimes obsessive thoughts and compulsive behaviors. If harm thoughts are occurring only during manic episodes, then bipolar disorder may be a more useful diagnosis because the treatments for that disorder may alleviate the temporary symptoms that look like OCD.

- **Psychotic symptoms:** Psychosis is probably the scariest word in the English language for people with Harm OCD. No matter how carefully I choose my words here, some readers are going to get reassured and others are going to get triggered. Neither are more likely than the other to be psychotic.

Psychosis is a term that loosely means an inability to distinguish between what is real and what is not. Naturally, people with OCD *all* struggle with some confusion over whether something is real, important, or true, but this in no way makes them psychotic. Psychotic features of the mind typically include delusions (very firmly fixed beliefs about things that are untrue or impossible) or hallucinations (visual or aural experiences occurring in the mind that are viewed as coming from outside the mind). In psychotic disorders, it is not the thought itself of harm that causes distress, but these delusions and hallucinations. Further, in psychosis there is an abnormally low willingness to accept further evidence about a belief. Note how this differs from OCD, where one is excessively *seeking out* evidence to prove that harming thoughts are not true.

People with Harm OCD are typically *not* struggling with psychotic features, but often worry that they are. On occasion, people with OCD who may have extremely low insight or absent insight (meaning, they view their fearful thoughts as reasonable but in some way still unwanted and intrusive) may cross over from obsession to delusional beliefs about the likelihood of losing control. At the higher end of severity of OCD with extremely low insight, this can be difficult to assess (especially to self-assess), so a thorough psychiatric evaluation can be helpful in these cases. If your treatment provider brings up psychotic features or antipsychotic medication, this does not automatically mean you are schizophrenic, nor that you have another psychotic disorder. It is important to remember that having some of these features does not mean you don't have OCD and does not mean you are actually going to harm anyone. It simply means that there may be additional psychiatric and therapeutic strategies for addressing your OCD and getting that insight back on track.

If you relate to any of the statements above, that doesn't mean that you *don't* also have OCD or that you are doomed to some unwanted diagnosis. The point of considering these challenges is to understand that it is wise to go into detail with a professional and to collaborate with that professional to obtain the best understanding of your symptoms so you can choose the best therapeutic approach. You may disclose a thought or an experience that at first sounds like a personality disorder or suicidality or psychosis of some kind, but then through careful back-and-forth with the clinician you may both conclude that this is not the case. It is important to give yourself and the clinician time to explore how you experience and relate to the thoughts, not just what the thoughts are.

Too many people get misdiagnosed either because they are seeing an untrained clinician or they are not articulating their symptoms in a way that allows the clinician to understand what is going on. This can unfortunately lead to nightmarish scenarios wherein people are unnecessarily hospitalized or erroneously reported to an authority as a safety concern. But it is also true that underdiagnosing can lead to other problems, and not just problems of harm. For example, people doing their best to fight OCD who don't know that they are bipolar may be doing everything right, but still find themselves going back to square one every few weeks or months and thinking that they are a failure when in fact they are simply having a manic episode that is causing a flareup of obsessive symptoms. Ultimately, what's important is that things that are *not* OCD have been ruled out or identified so that OCD treatment can move forward at its most effective.

Okay, so that was uncomfortable. You're uncomfortable reading about all the ways you could potentially not have OCD or also have some problem you don't want. I'm uncomfortable because I just wrote all the reasons people are probably going to email me reassurance-seeking questions or be upset with me for triggering their worst fears. Now that we've both acknowledged our discomfort, let's move forward.

You're Not Crazy

I'm going to remind you of this throughout the book. "Crazy" is a nonsense word we use to put ourselves down when we don't like what we see in the mind. You have a common, diag-nosable, treatable disorder. This disorder necessarily involves obsessions, and the content of your obsessions happens to focus on issues related to harm. You view these issues as con-taminants of the mind and use compulsions to clean them from your mind. The problem is that this doesn't work. The more you mentally wash, the dirtier your brain thinks you are. This process of negative reinforcement is actually the opposite of crazy. You *should* be more likely to repeat things that are reinforced and it's normal to seek out behaviors you think will reduce your pain. "Disorder" simply means out of order, where the behaviors have become so excessive that they cause more problems. We look at these issues as mental health issues because we have reason to believe that features of the brain may make you more likely to find unwanted thoughts less tol-erable, to feel alarmed by their presence, and to overthink that alarm. Understanding these predispositions is an important first step in understanding how to overcome them.

Recap

Okay, one chapter down and you're still here. You did a great job taking in a lot of technical psychology concepts, some of which might have been really triggering. Don't worry if it didn't immediately click for you. I just want to set a sturdy platform here so we can build on it as we look deeper into how to overcome your Harm OCD. So what was chapter 1 all about? OCD is a common and treatable mental health condition characterized by obsessions and compulsions. Obsessions are unwanted intrusive thoughts, feelings, and sensations. Compulsions are physical or mental behaviors aimed at reducing anxiety about these intrusions. A significant number of people with OCD have obsessions related to the fear of harming self or others and having unwanted violent thoughts. Why we have violent thoughts (and why we notice them) are not easy questions to answer since there may be evolutionary/biological, psychological, or behavioral reasons for them arising. But whatever may precede them, simply *having* violent thoughts is a normal part of the human experience. There are, however, other mental health conditions that can sometimes be associated with violent thoughts, so getting a proper assessment and diagnosis is important. Now let's take a look at what tools you can use to overcome your Harm OCD.

CHAPTER 2

Tools and Techniques

No doubt you've been working hard trying to get rid of your unwanted violent thoughts. This hard work hasn't paid off, so you came here. Now you find yourself considering *another* kind of hard work. If you're scared that the tools that lie ahead won't do the trick, that's perfectly normal. It's okay to go at your own pace, and if you want to just read this chapter like it's a textbook without thinking too hard about actually using these tools yourself, that's okay too. I'm going to go over four basic OCD-fighting tools in general terms here, then in part 2 I'll show in more detail how they can be applied to specific Harm OCD manifestations.

Uncertainty Acceptance and Harm OCD

Pick up any book on OCD and it will tell you that thoughts are just thoughts and you don't need to worry about what they mean, because they don't inherently mean anything. This reassuring (and true) statement may still not be particularly satisfying. The disorder makes it difficult to sit with the discomfort of letting a thought simply be a thought when it feels like it could be a threat of harm. In the previous chapter, I mentioned how defending yourself in an argument against OCD validates OCD's claim that an argument is worth having. If in the presence of an unwanted violent thought you repeatedly state to yourself, "It's just a thought, it's just a thought, it's just a thought..." then you are simultaneously admitting that OCD's claim (that it is *more* than a thought) is worth disproving. To overcome this, you need to enhance your willingness to accept uncertainty about the thought. In other words, you have to remain open to the idea that the thought may be something more than a thought, and that you are simply choosing not to do much about it.

Plead the Fifth

When you have Harm OCD, it can often feel like you're repeatedly being accused of a terrible crime. OCD is your accuser, but it also acts like a high-powered defense attorney who says, "Look, I can get you a not-guilty plea, guaranteed. I'm going to get all the witnesses and all the evidence and bring it all up in your trial and if you stick with me, the jury will acquit you. 100%." You hear this and think, *Great, let's do this. I know I'm not guilty, let's make sure it's official.* Then the OCD says, "Sure thing. By the way, I cost $1000/hour, I bill 24 hours a day, and the case will take a few years, maybe more. In the end, you'll get your not-guilty verdict, probably, but I should tell you, the long trial will decimate you and the verdict might not make much of a difference. But never mind that, let's get to that evidence of your innocence."

An OCD therapist like me is no high-powered attorney. I'm more like a pubic defender and my advice is simple: Plead the fifth. In an American court, when you plead the fifth amendment to the U.S. constitution, you are saying that you will not answer a question that could incriminate you. In other words, no matter what the OCD asks, just don't answer. You're probably thinking, "No, that makes me look really guilty." Then I explain, "If you don't take the bait and answer OCD's questions, this thing will go to mistrial in a week. No one will remember it. It might as well have been just a forgettable fluke." This approach is what it means to accept uncertainty, and it is indeed scary. It doesn't come with that shiny promise of complete vindication. But it also doesn't cost you a lifetime of obsessing. Accepting uncertainty about your violent thoughts means allowing the possibility that they could be true by not trying to prove otherwise.

But what if? you say. *What if this thought means something about me? What if this thought is a sign of future behavior? What if I wanted it or will act on it?* Jonathan Grayson, in his influential book *Freedom from Obsessive Compulsive Disorder*, argues that "the core of OCD is trying to get rid of uncertainty in our lives in an attempt to be 100% certain" (2003, 8). The questions above feel like they must be answered and yet none of them could possibly ever be answered with 100% certainty. They are, by definition, ideas about *potential*. Part of the cruelty of Harm OCD is this internal demand to know perfectly something that could never be known—what will happen in the future (will I hurt someone?), what were my intentions (did I want to cause harm?), and what does this actually mean (do these thoughts make me capable of harm?)?

Unhelpful Ideas About Uncertainty Acceptance

You may be asking yourself: *How can I accept uncertainty about a thought such as stabbing myself or pushing a loved one over a railing? Wouldn't that make me some kind of a monster or at the very least reduce me to being miserable in the knowledge that my fears could be true?* The answer to these questions is surprisingly simple: *No*. Accepting uncertainty is not accepting defeat. Accepting uncertainty is a power position. It says, "I need no defense and my feet are planted in such a way that no gust of wind can knock me down." So why is uncertainty acceptance so hard?

MISTAKEN BELIEF 1: UNCERTAINTY MEANS FIFTY-FIFTY

Obsessions often begin with the words "What if" and follow with some description of an event the thinker finds intolerable. What if I snap and harm a loved one? What if I am a closeted sociopath? What if I just jump off the roof? Compulsions are designed to increase certainty about these unwanted outcomes. Using the above examples, a person might avoid being alone with a triggering loved one, spend hours researching the term "sociopath" on the Internet, or ruminate over reasons why he or she would never jump from a building. Since these compulsive efforts never really work in the end, you are still left with only one option—accepting uncertainty that the feared concept could be true. But accepting uncertainty does not mean accepting that there is a "one out of two" shot that your fear could be true. The odds of a random person spontaneously snapping or losing his or her identity are of course very low. The odds of the ceiling falling on my head as I write this are also very low. Nonetheless, the odds are higher than zero. Surely getting up on this chair and pushing on the ceiling to make sure it's secure would be a strange use of my time. Yet ceilings can and do collapse. So what I have to do in order to finish this sentence is admit that a calculation *could* be done and I am simply choosing not to do it. This doesn't suddenly mean that the ceiling is either going to fall or not fall at the flip of a coin or that I should sit here thinking that my life is on the line. It means that I am letting myself behave in a manner consistent with the odds being very low.

MISTAKEN BELIEF 2: THERE ARE THINGS WE CANNOT ACCEPT UNCERTAINTY ABOUT

You may assume, *Sure, I can be uncertain if my hands are clean, but how can I live without being certain that I'm not going to murder someone?* This belief betrays a poor understanding of the nature of certainty and how it differs from confidence. Mostly, we use the word *certainty* interchangeably with the word *confidence*. Confidence is a feeling. It is a *sense* that, given certain conditions, certain experiences are predictable. As I sit in this chair, I feel certain that it will support my weight, but in fact I am not certain. I am confident. Embracing this difference between the feeling of confidence and the fantasy state of certainty is easy when the consequences seem tolerable. Worst-case scenario, the chair beneath me crumbles and I have a good "How I got that butt bruise" story. But envisioning a world in which you somehow cope with the outcomes of your violent fears coming true is not so easy. This gets translated as a reason to commit to compulsive behavior because you feel you simply *have* to, because there appears to be no way uncertainty about *this* issue could be tolerated.

The problem is, certainty still doesn't exist. OCD doesn't care how brutal the content of the thoughts are. Certainty remains a constant. Only confidence exists and compulsions are the very thing that deplete confidence. Compulsions send the message to the brain: "Warning: confidence is lacking." We must accept uncertainty about all things, not because all things are likely or even worth any attention at all, but because we have no alternative. When confidence is absent, we can find it by choosing the behaviors confident people choose (for example, not paying much attention to our unwanted thoughts and instead engaging with life in the present).

MISTAKEN BELIEF 3: PEOPLE WITH OCD ARE NOT AS GOOD AT ACCEPTING UNCERTAINTY

You may struggle to tolerate uncertainty about your harm thoughts, but this does not mean you have a general deficit in the area of uncertainty tolerance. Because OCD sufferers often see things in finer detail and become aware of what others might consider "fringe" thoughts that don't typically demand attention, they may feel like they experience more *ideas* that require one to be uncertain about. In other words, OCD sufferers are spending significantly more time actively and consciously accepting uncertainty, and doing it *well*, than people who aren't even noticing the things we have to accept uncertainty about. It is only when the focus of attention is on a particular *obsession* that people with OCD struggle to accept uncertainty.

It is not unusual for a client to come to my office to work on a fear of stabbing because he struggles to cope with the uncertainty that he could harm someone or harm himself if he held a knife. But how did he get to my office? Presumably he drove a metal death cage on wheels at sixty miles per hour surrounded by others (of unknown levels of driving skill) doing the same thing. So accepting serious life-or-death uncertainties is not the problem. Accepting uncertainty about your *obsession* is the problem. OCD sufferers are actually uncertainty-accepting pros. You notice what others don't and you allow things to be as they are more often than not. The trick is learning how to generalize this skill to apply to your specific obsessions, instead of only to the plethora of other thoughts on the radar.

MISTAKEN BELIEF 4: ACCEPTING UNCERTAINTY MEANS YOU CAN'T ASSUME THE BEST

There is a myth that OCD promotes in the mind that you don't deserve to be happy; that if you're happy, it must be the result of not paying enough attention to something important. So if you try to do what happy people do, you may feel an urge to neutralize that with self-criticism or self-punishment of some kind. Accepting uncertainty is not a mandate to assume the worst and then dwell on it. Rather than it having to be a net negative experience, it can be a freeing one. If you assume that your fears are untrue and engage in behaviors that reflect this, it still leaves space for the possibility that you are wrong.

Accepting uncertainty can mean living joyfully with the assumption that your fears are *not* true, that your OCD is a glitch at best, or a liar and bully at its worst. If you have a thought about pushing a stranger in front of a bus and you walk right by that stranger with a smile and resist the urge to look back to make sure you haven't harmed him, then this is living as if your thoughts are nonsense. If you have a thought about poisoning yourself for no reason and you say, "Well, that's interesting" and then leave a bottle of bleach sitting out in the laundry room, then again, this is living with the assumption that your fears are not true. This is not because you reassured yourself or proved anything, but because you've chosen a behavioral path consistent with a healthy assumption instead of a compulsive one.

Now that we've looked at some ideas that get in the way of uncertainty acceptance, let's take a look at the tools that enhance your uncertainty acceptance skills.

Cognitive Approaches

The first tool we can use to accept uncertainty and resist compulsions is examining the way we are thinking about the things that trigger us. If we understand that compulsions are the problem, then it would seem that treating OCD is really simple—choose not to do compulsions. But even when you understand the voluntary nature of a compulsion, it really doesn't seem that way at the time. One reason may be the *way* you are thinking at the time you get triggered—not *what* you are thinking, but *how*. As you approach a triggering situation (that is, an obsession is brought on), you may have every intention to resist compulsions, but something in the way you are thinking about the situation pushes you over the edge and seems to remove choice from the equation. This *way* of thinking is called a cognitive distortion.

Common Cognitive Distortions in Harm OCD

Cognitive distortions are thoughts or ways of thinking that cause us to perceive reality inaccurately (Burns 1989). In the context of OCD, these bent lenses of the mind trick us into overestimating the risks and responsibilities we associate with our unwanted thoughts. Let's take a look at just some of the thinking errors you are most likely to encounter in your fight against Harm OCD. This is by no means an official list of all of the possible cognitive distortions, just a small handful that may stand out especially in Harm OCD.

Thought-Action Fusion (TAF): This means believing that the presence of a thought either changes the likelihood of the thought becoming true (probability TAF) or that having a thought is, in and of itself, equivalent to an immoral bad act (morality TAF) (Rachman and Shafran 1999). You could say that all Harm OCD is a problem of thought-action fusion. After all, if you didn't hold the mistaken belief that your violent thoughts are going to bring about a danger to self or others or that your violent thoughts were a threat to your moral identity, you wouldn't think of yourself as having violent obsessions in the first place. If you struggle with probability TAF, you may feel that you have to do compulsions to avoid the guilt that arises when you consider you may have harmed or be about to harm someone. If you struggle with morality TAF, you may feel that you have to do compulsions to escape the shame of negative self-judgment that comes with believing you are a bad person for having bad thoughts. Both may be in play. Being able to recognize when your compulsive behavior is being driven by the mere presence of your violent thoughts can help you step back and remember: Thoughts and actions are not the same thing.

Catastrophizing: This means predicting a negative future *and* assuming you can't cope with it. Understanding catastrophizing in the context of Harm OCD can be tricky. Of course what you're thinking is catastrophic, and of course coping with it seems impossible! The thing to understand about this way of thinking is simply that we cannot predict the future. This does not mean we have to assume the future is bad, or even that there is a fifty-fifty chance that it will be bad (recall the discussion on uncertainty from earlier in this chapter). What it means is that when we allow OCD to trick us into thinking we know something about the future, it makes it easier for OCD to bully us into doing compulsions. Further, because we cannot predict the future, we also do not know how our fears coming true will actually affect us, and thus we do not know how we will cope. People often derive great strength from tragic and humbling circumstances. So when we recognize that we are predicting the future, we can note that, step back, and reintroduce choice to the equation.

Discounting the Positive: The universe is already constantly providing you with evidence that you and your thoughts are not dangerous. You likely have a long history of not causing harm, which is, in part, why you find it so disturbing to have these harming thoughts at all. But when the thought occurs that you've had all these violent thoughts during all this time and still you haven't laid hands on anyone, you discount it, you push it away. You do it with "oh but this time" thinking. The hundred other times you ate with a knife and fork and nobody got hurt mean nothing to you. It's *this* time that you're worried about. It's always *this* time. Being able to notice this "oh but this time" thinking can be a useful way to remember to resist compulsions.

Tunnel Vision: The inverse of discounting the positive can be seen here. With one hand you push away fundamentally reassuring information that your life history indicates no violent intent and with the other you collect evidence to support the OCD theory that you are a harm to self or others. Tunnel vision is a way of thinking in which you pull in information from your surroundings to support the obsession and lose sight of the fact that what you are noticing in your surroundings is being noticed simply because, well, that's your thing. You are likely not only to notice things related to your harm obsessions, but also to notice that you *noticed* it. It's at this moment that the OCD says, "See? You noticed that thought/knife/person/etc. because you're gonna do something bad!" When we are obsessed, we are stuck in a tunnel with our obsessions and we see little else outside that tunnel.

Emotional Reasoning: This way of thinking occurs when we use feelings as the primary evidence for a belief. For example, you might feel anxious when you're around your child and conclude, "Because I feel anxious, this must be a sign that I am going to harm her." The problem with using feelings as primary evidence is that feelings are unreliable. You may feel anxious for a lot of reasons, including no reason. Similarly, you may feel guilty and let this experience drive you to review your past to see if you've harmed anyone. But you have OCD, so you feel guilty a lot, often without knowing why. If we let our emotions determine when we do or do not do compulsions, we invite the OCD to manipulate our emotions to get us to do compulsions. It's not that we should avoid or ignore all of our feelings all of the time, but we get a competitive edge over OCD when we choose not to let emotions be the *primary* reason for engaging in behaviors.

Shoulds: The word "should" usually represents some useful guideline. You probably *should* wash your hands after using the toilet. This is a generally accepted practice and applies pretty equally to all of us (except if you are doing exposure therapy for a fear of unclean hands). Okay, so what if you use the toilet and then learn that there is a bomb in the building? Should you wash your hands or deprioritize hygiene just for now? This may seem like a goofy analogy, but quite often in OCD, "should" statements become so rigid that you can find yourself rationalizing compulsive behavior to the exclusion of significantly more important things. If you are carrying around a thought process like *I should never have violent thoughts* and then you become aware of a violent thought, you may feel the urge to drop whatever you were doing before the thought popped up and start ritualizing. But what you were doing may have been important. *Anything* you are doing in reality is objectively more important than what you are doing in your head. Recognizing when you are using *should* statements as a justification for compulsions can be a useful tool in catching and abandoning those compulsions.

Cognitive approaches to OCD are about learning a language to help you understand how the OCD is trying to communicate its demand for compulsions. Like any language, you'll have many words that mean the same or similar things. But being able to call your thinking by *any* term is a step toward positioning yourself as an observer instead of a victim. From that position, you can challenge OCD's claim that you must do compulsions.

Cognitive Restructuring

Challenging OCD on the cognitive level can be delicate work. The more we engage with the content of our thoughts, the easier it is to fall for the trap of believing it's all about content. However, if you can recognize that your thinking is distorted, then you can ask what it would look like without that distortion. What you're doing is deconstructing the faulty thinking and reorganizing it as rational thinking.

This approach is called cognitive restructuring. It's important to remember here that we are not using cognitive restructuring to challenge the *probability* of your thoughts being true. That just feeds into the OCD by validating its false claims as worth arguing over. Instead, we use restructuring to reach an objective viewpoint by challenging "overvalued beliefs about responsibility, about the meaning and importance of thought, and about the meaning of thought control" (Purdon 2004, 1174).

In other words, we are choosing to sit with uncertainty because we are not confused about having to do something different. Mostly this means admitting what we don't know. As one example, consider the difference between saying to yourself that you must do a compulsion because if you don't, someone will get hurt, and simply saying to yourself that you can't predict the future, but in your experience, compulsions make your life worse. In part 2 of this book, I'll show you tips for challenging distorted thinking in specific Harm OCD manifestations.

Exposure and Response Prevention (ERP)

One of my favorite movies is the 1986 remake of *The Fly*. If you tell a woman you're breaking up with her because you're turning into a giant mutant fly and are afraid you'll harm her if she sticks around anyway, well, that's true love. The tagline on the poster for this movie says, "Be Afraid. Be Very Afraid." My recommendation for treating your OCD is to be afraid, but just be, er, *kinda* afraid. Exposure and response prevention (ERP) is not just some torture game invented by twisted therapists to make your life worse. It can be a very effective tool in the treatment of harm obsessions (Abramowitz et al. 2003a). Gradually confronting the things you are afraid of while resisting the urge to do negatively reinforcing rituals is how you break the obsessive-compulsive cycle. Only through that can we learn to accept, or even embrace, uncertainty, and only then can we find peace in the mind. But how do we get good at catching and resisting compulsions? In the few pages that preceded this, we looked at ways in which we get tricked by distorted thinking into forgetting that compulsions are voluntary. Here we will look at how to practice resisting compulsions by bringing up the urge to do them and facing them down instead of giving in.

Habituation and Inhibitory Learning

What do we mean when we say ERP *works*? What exactly is working and how is it different from, well, not working? Our current understanding of what happens when we confront our scary thoughts and uncomfortable feelings can be divided into two categories: feeling better and getting better at feeling.

FEELING BETTER—HABITUATION

Having Harm OCD is like having a horror movie playing in the cinema of your head on repeat. To make matters worse, if you try not to think of it or you try to shut it off, its persistence only becomes more upsetting. However, if you watch the same horror movie enough times and really stay with it, you may stop feeling afraid over time. You may feel bored as your brain starts to respond to the imagery with, *Oh, that again.* This process is called *habituation*, which is another way of saying that your brain gets so used to you disregarding the alarm that it pulls the plug on it. Consider that feeling anxious and upset takes energy and you have a limited supply of this. Your brain delivers this energy in order to push you to avoid being harmed by whatever is threatening you. Your brain can learn to stop providing you energy for this purpose if it appears to be going to no use. In short, habituation is feeling less fear in the presence of the same trigger.

GETTING BETTER AT FEELING—INHIBITORY LEARNING

Focusing exclusively on habituation (getting rid of fear) can result in developing an unhealthy aversion to fear itself, leading to the erroneous conclusion that if you don't habituate in ERP, you have failed (Jacoby and Abramowitz 2016). Some horror movies just have a way of getting under our skin. No matter how many times we watch them, they still make us cringe. This is done by design, not by accident. Interestingly enough, this is one of the reasons an avid horror enthusiast might give for identifying this as a great movie. "A hundred viewings and it still makes me freaked out!" In this case, what happens is the fear stops being an indicator of something bad (a hundred times the fear came up and a hundred times nothing happened) and starts being something that is simply experienced in the context that it is in.

Put differently, the first time you see something scary, you learn a fear response. People with OCD get locked in to this response and begin to believe that the fear is fundamentally intolerable; so even when you do ERP, you may habituate for a while (get away from feeling fear) only to find yourself afraid again down the road. Still, ERP seems to *work* in the sense that when people commit to it, their lives become less burdened by OCD. The reason for this is that ERP causes the brain to learn to *inhibit* the fear response and allow other responses to also take place (Craske et al. 2008). So people who watch horror films multiple times may continue to notice the scary bits (the fear response), but their attention to this competes with everything else they begin to notice, such as the makeup effects, the set design, the acting, the music, *and* both the absence of being harmed and the belief that the fear is tolerable. So you may spit out your popcorn at the movies when the monster jumps into the frame, but your drive to leave the cinema and run for safety is inhibited. Your brain says, *Yeah, it's really scary, just roll with it anyway.* This phenomenon is called *inhibitory learning.*

Stepping away from the movie metaphor, let's review these two concepts above in Harm OCD terms. Imagine your Harm OCD tells you that it is not safe to be around a kitchen knife and a loved one at the same time. You have an obsessive fear that under these conditions you may "snap" and stab your loved one. This idea causes you a great amount of discomfort and makes being in the kitchen with your loved one extremely fear-inducing. ERP would involve exposing yourself to those conditions while resisting compulsions (which might include hiding or avoiding the knife, seeking reassurance about whether or not you could snap, mentally checking to see if you would or wouldn't snap, and so on). Exposure might include anything from looking at a picture of a knife or writing a story about harming someone with a knife, all the way up to standing in the kitchen holding the knife close to your loved one. For ERP to be effective, this has to be done in the absence of compulsions, with the focus on accepting uncertainty, not disproving your fears. Over time, you may *habituate* to the conditions (feel better, find the whole thing silly and easily tolerated) and/or you may *inhibit* your fear response by associating the experience with cooking, shared experiences with your loved one, and the belief that the fear is tolerable (and worth it).

Different Ways to Do ERP

The pain and sense of isolation that may come with your unwanted violent thoughts may leave you assuming that your obsession doesn't lend itself to ERP. You may have even had a therapist with little or no training in OCD treatment tell you that exposure won't work with violent obsessions: "How will you do it? We can't risk you hurting yourself or others!" This couldn't be further from the truth. In fact, because so much of Harm OCD resides in the mind (you may be afraid of sharp objects, but you're also afraid of your thoughts), there are actually many different ways to do effective exposure for harm fears. Some Harm OCD exposures can be done *in vivo* (exposing yourself to real-life situations and triggers) and some can be done as imaginal exposures (creating stories about feared events). For any exposure, it is important to stay within the following three rules:

- **Don't do exposure in a manner where accidental harm is likely to take place.** Remember, the purpose of exposure is to challenge the distorted belief that you are incapable of tolerating uncertainty about your harm-related thoughts and feelings. There is no reason ERP should include risk-taking behaviors that fall outside of generally understood safety principles. In other words, we don't expose to a fear of causing a car accident by driving blind-folded or intoxicated. We do take the risk of driving, with a seatbelt, at a reasonable speed, and with our disturbing thoughts, but without compulsions.

- **You don't have to violate your values in the name of ERP.** Nothing about ERP demands that you violate your personal moral or ethical code. Your OCD may make you feel doubtful about that code and its integrity, so this is understandably scary to consider. But the point is that ERP does not ask you to harm anyone or engage in any particular behavior you believe to be inherently wrong. When doing ERP, you might want to ask yourself whether the feeling of immorality is coming from your values or from your OCD. For example, allowing yourself to have scary thoughts while using a knife to peel an apple in the same room as a loved one may *feel* immoral, as if you were using this innocent person as a guinea pig in a sick experiment. But using a knife to cut an apple in someone's presence does not itself (presumably) go against your values.

- **No testing.** For many, this is the hardest rule to stick to, but it makes a huge difference. Testing, or checking to be certain about your feelings *about* the exposure, renders the exposure useless. Trying to prove that you won't harm yourself or others or trying to prove that you're not a "bad" person only interferes with your ability to expose yourself to uncertainty and teaches the brain that your tests are valid assessments of reality. Extreme checking, making extraordinary strides to get certain that your harm thoughts won't come true (recall the discussion on this from chapter 1), may look like ERP at times, but it is in fact a problematic compulsion that will worsen your symptoms and is not a treatment strategy.

I will come back to these ERP rules as applied to more specific Harm OCD concerns in chapters 3-6. Now let's take a look at different exposure approaches you can employ.

In Vivo Exposure

This means doing ERP to real circumstances you may be avoiding because of your Harm OCD. This could include exposure to driving, to windows (if you fear jumping), to knives, or to other things you see as threatening. It could include purposely being around people who are triggering. More than just being around these triggering objects or people, in vivo ERP involves interacting with them. For example, you could be using a pair of scissors for an art project while allowing yourself to have thoughts about stabbing yourself with them, or going for a walk with a triggering person where there may not be someone else to observe you to make sure you do not cause harm.

Additionally, to get on top of any kind of Harm OCD, the first thing you need to do is identify and reduce safety behaviors. If you have knives, pills, and so on locked away so that you don't impulsively use them to cause harm, then you need to get them out in plain view as soon as you can. If you recall from the description of the obsessive-compulsive cycle in chapter 1, our compulsive behaviors actually reinforce the connection between obsessions, our beliefs about them, and how we feel we must respond to them. Naturally, the presence of harm thoughts can be discomforting and, therefore, you are initially driven to avoid that discomfort. Yet at the same time, when we avoid things, we send a message to the brain that those things are dangerous. To turn this around, we need to interact with the things we feel compelled to avoid and send a message to the brain that these things are not the threats they appear to be. We do this not by giving ourselves reassurances, but by demonstrating it with our behavior. The endgame is not to prove the obsession away, but to stop resisting the uncertainty regarding its content.

For example, a person with unwanted thoughts about harming children may feel compelled to avoid walking down a street near a school where children may be present. In vivo exposure and response prevention here would be to purposely walk down that street and allow whatever thoughts and feelings this elicits to come along for the walk. Remember, it is of utmost importance here that this not be looked at as a testing exercise, an opportunity to see how you handle the thoughts or to prove to yourself that you won't harm a child. The message you are trying to send to your brain here is that you are capable of walking along the street in the presence of children *and* in the presence of the thoughts that they trigger *without* responding compulsively. That is how you get the brain to tag these thoughts as meaningless chatter. If they are not worthy of arguing with, they are not worth worrying about.

Imaginal Exposure

This means doing exposure in your mind. You may find your imagination a nuisance because you keep imagining terrible things, but here you can use it to your advantage. This can be done alongside in vivo exposure, such as sitting next to someone while imagining harming that person, or it can be done separately, as in writing a narrative describing your harm thoughts becoming real. For many with Harm OCD, the line between in vivo and imaginal exposure is blurry. If you are afraid that having violent thoughts could lead to violent actions, then imagining violent actions is both in vivo (confronting the actual feared experience) and imaginal (envisioning the feared experience occurring). Using the example above, while doing the in vivo exposure of walking near children when they trigger your harm thoughts, you might also include the imaginal exposure of telling yourself that you could harm one of them, or purposely picturing yourself harming them (again, no testing). Telling stories in your head without slipping into mental rituals can be a difficult task. You may find it easier to resist compulsions when doing imaginal exposure in written form. Let's take a look at some written imaginal exposure techniques, also knows as *scripts*.

Acceptance and Motivation Scripts

Harm OCD has a way of blindsiding you with such grotesque and offensive intrusive thoughts that it's easy to forget that resisting compulsions is number one on your agenda. To be consistent in standing up to your Harm OCD, you need to first accept that you really have these unwanted thoughts and that you really are about to confront uncertainty about them to overcome it. It's completely normal to find this idea to be overwhelming and to doubt your ability to rise to the challenge. To stay motivated, you can write a script that lays out what you're honestly signing up for in the fight against OCD.

In the section below, I've written out the format for an acceptance and motivation script. You can read through this and try it on your own later, or you can pull out a piece of paper and get to work on one now. You will also get another chance to explore this technique throughout part 2 of this book.

My Acceptance and Motivation Script

A good to way to construct this exercise is to write out the four questions that follow, then take some notes on what you think the answers are, then put it together into one four-paragraph script.

Question 1: What behaviors am I going to change?

Write out a list of all of the ways you try to get certainty about your violent thoughts and state assertively that you are going to cease them. Don't worry if you find this hard to believe just yet or you don't feel ready to stop all of your compulsions this very moment. Just state what they are and that you are going to change them. Think of statements like "I am going to stop avoiding the knife drawer" or "I am going to start going to the top floor of the building."

Question 2: What unwanted consequences am I risking?

Write out a list of all of the terrible things you can imagine happening as a result of stopping compulsions. This can be as straightforward as saying that you might harm a specific person or as abstract as saying you might be driven mad by never getting the answers. Writing this may be scary, but the point is to be honest with yourself about how hard it is to take the risk of getting better so that when you do, you do so with real purpose. Keep all of your language in uncertainty, using words like might, may, or could, instead of will. Instead of saying "I worry that xyz will happen if I stop my compulsions," try to push yourself to more assertively state "Because I am stopping my compulsions, xyz may happen…"

Question 3: What is the likely outcome of continuing to obey the OCD?

Try to imagine putting no effort into fighting OCD. Picture yourself as a perfect slave to the disorder, devoting 100% of your attention to the pursuit of certainty about your unwanted thoughts. Describe in detail what this would actually look like. Include the costs of this behavior, both the literal financial ones (not being able to work, being hospitalized, and so on) and the more abstract ones (the heartbreak your decline would cause your loved ones). The point is to demonstrate the unacceptability of life with untreated Harm OCD. End your list with the statement that you will still not have the certainty you are seeking despite your extreme efforts. You can use certainty language here, such as *will* and *going to*.

Question 4: What do I value that makes it worth it for me to fight my Harm OCD?

Think about what kind of person your OCD tells you that you are. Now think about what kind of person you suspect you probably *really* are. They're quite different. Who are you such that you would be willing to fight OCD when doing so is this scary? What's it worth to you to get back to being that person? What kind of spouse, sibling, parent, professional, and so on do you believe yourself to really be when unburdened by your Harm OCD? Given these qualities, and the fact that compulsions don't work, why is it worth it for you to make these changes and fight your OCD?

Once you have your completed document, you can read it daily to help point you in the right direction. You can also edit it however you see fit to enhance it over time. The important thing is to make sure you hit all four points and keep them present in your mind:

1. You are going to stand up to OCD by changing specific behaviors.

2. Changing these behaviors is scary because you believe it *could* result in your fears coming true.

3. Staying the same means living as a slave to perpetually worsening OCD.

4. It is worth it to change your behavior and accept uncertainty about your fears because of who you are and what you really care about.

Flooding Scripts

If you think about why you do compulsions at all, it's not an exclusively intellectual exercise. Wanting to prove that you won't cause harm is only part of the equation. Alongside these disgusting thoughts is a feeling. It might be different for everyone, but most of my clients describe it as dread, guilt, terror, or some combination of the three. So compulsions often arise from a desperate attempt to get painful feelings to subside, even temporarily. If we keep our eye on the ball here (stop compulsions), then exposure strategies that help us habituate to or make space for these feelings can be an excellent tool. What I am calling "flooding scripts" here involves writing out a description of thoughts and events in such a way that they elicit the same (or worse) feelings you get when your become aware of your unwanted thoughts. The aim is to generate the urge to do compulsions for the purpose of practicing being *in* that urge *without* doing those compulsions. Here's a template that might be effective (you can do this now or continue reading through and practice this another time):

- Describe your OCD's claim as if it were fact. Start with an affirmation or admission, as in "I am going to do xyz" or "these thoughts mean xyz" or "I am doing xyz." Don't let on that you have a fear about it or suffer from a common disorder like OCD. Just go straight to what the OCD is saying and agree with it. "I am going to snap and kill my daughter with a knife," for example.

- Describe what happens when you act on your thoughts or when your fears otherwise come true. What happens in that moment that you snap and go over the edge? Describe the victim of your violence (even if the victim is you) and the experience that victim has as a result of your fear coming true.

- Describe the consequences of these actions in the long term and how they ultimately impact your legacy in a way that you find unacceptable.

Remember, in this kind of scripting, we're not interested in uncertainty or in the *truth* of the thoughts. We're focused only on generating uncomfortable feelings for the purpose of learning how to feel them without doing compulsions. This script does not have to make a ton of sense or follow a specific chronology. All that matters is that it generates the *feeling of* needing to do compulsions and that the script does not contain within it any reassurance or other attempts to argue with the OCD. You may be thinking that you're already feeling this pain on a daily basis, so it's redundant to go out of your way to generate it, but consider that this exercise is about choosing to have the feelings and not about trying to defend yourself from them or simply put up with them.

You can write a fresh script daily, write a template script and read it often each day, or write a script and record and listen to it repeatedly. It's perfectly understandable that you may not want this script to fall into the wrong hands. It's going to be pretty nasty stuff and, out of context, it could be alarming to someone who comes across it by accident. If this is a particular concern of yours, the script is just as effective if you destroy it after each writing. A good flooding script is the mental equivalent of touching a dumpster when you're afraid of germs and keeping your hand there as long as it takes to stop feeling overwhelmed. Remember, all that matters for this tool to be effective is that it generates an urge to do compulsions and that you aim to sit with that urge rather than sate it.

Speaking of sitting…

Mindfulness and Harm OCD

While ERP is the gold standard of OCD treatment, and indeed the best way to become of master at resisting compulsions and accepting uncertainty, finding the right mindset for this arduous task may be difficult. You're already getting hammered on a regular basis by horrifying thoughts, sickening guilt, and debilitating anxiety. OCD uses this to lead you around aimlessly through what feels like the never-ending expanse of outer space. But what if instead of being lost in space with your OCD, you could position yourself seated in a planetarium looking up at the stars and directing your own attention? This skill of being able to view thoughts as thoughts and rest your awareness on what *is*, instead of on what *could be*, is called mindfulness.

Sharks in the Aquarium

Here in the Baltimore area we have a terrific National Aquarium. After you make your way through the tropical fish, the frogs, the jellyfish, and so on, you get to my favorite part, the sharks. The tour ends with a series of ramps that work their way down to a circular aquarium below. The lights are dim and ominous *Jaws*-esque music emanates from hidden speakers. If you stand in front of any window, a shark will eventually swim by. Because the aquarium is circular, the shark will eventually swim by your window again if you stay in the same place. The funny thing is, even though it is clear that you're not in any danger, the combination of the lighting, the music, and the sheer creepiness of these creatures is kind of disturbing. But because you know you're not in harm's way on this side of the glass, you allow yourself to be disturbed. You also allow yourself to notice their beauty, the way they move, the different shapes they come in, and so on. They are more than just the thoughts and feelings they elicit.

Having OCD feels a lot like being in a shark tank with the sharks. When you see a shark coming at you, you don't just tread water and observe it. You scramble to get away. Your thoughts, like sharks, seem like they can destroy you. Mindfulness means remembering that you are not in the shark tank—you are in the aquarium. The shark may still be disturbing, but you allow the disturbance to come and go. When we are mindful, the harm thoughts are just individual sharks in the aquarium swimming by. The anxiety, fear, and disgust we experience with OCD are also just different kinds of sharks to watch. The physical sensations you associate with snapping or losing control—again, these are just sharks in the aquarium (maybe that weird one with a saw for a face). Self-critical thoughts about having harm obsessions? More sharks. When we identify with the mind and see ourselves as fused with our thoughts, we find ourselves in the shark tank. But when we remember to be *mindful*, we remember we are really just at the aquarium.

Right, but what if the glass breaks and the sharks come pouring out and eat my face while I'm drowning in a stew of fish feces and broken glass?

Okay, so mindfulness doesn't come easy, I know.

Mindfulness is the ability to observe your experiences as they are, in the present moment, and without judgment. The problem with OCD is that the disorder yanks your attention from the present and insists that you do compulsions and rituals in order to return. Developing your mindfulness skills can help improve your awareness of when you're being pulled from the present by your OCD and provide the tools for coming back to the present without having to do the compulsions or rituals. Mindfulness also enhances your ability to observe your thoughts, feelings, and sensations as they really *are*—as thoughts, feelings, and sensations.

Harm OCD triggers are often quick, sharp, and brutal, like the content of the associated thoughts. Because of this, sufferers coping with Harm OCD are likely to jump from what triggered them straight to some behavior that relieves the pain (a compulsion). But between the trigger and the compulsion is an experience. That experience includes what you think about the trigger and how it feels to want to neutralize it. When we skip over this middle part, however, we miss the opportunity to interfere in the obsessive-compulsive cycle. If we are mindful, by which I mean if we can stay present with the trigger, our experience of it, *and* the urge to do compulsions, then there is an opportunity to stand up to the OCD.

Understanding What a Mind Does

Consider that your mind is just whatever it is that you look through in order to see what's going on inside the brain. Your mind is like a flashlight that you point at different territories in a landscape made up of ideas, emotions, and sensations. You can have any kind of thought that is available to be had, and when you say you are having a *particular* thought, you mean you are shining the light on this idea in this present moment. Some thoughts are more pleasant to shine a light on than others. The problem with OCD is that if you identify areas of your mental landscape to be off limits, that's where the OCD goes.

The OCD wants one thing only, to dominate your attention so that you engage in compulsions. So it's no mystery that OCD plants its flag in the territory most offensive to you, the territory of causing harm. It adds insult to this injury by focusing the envisioned harm on the things you care the most about. If you try to avoid these territories, the OCD grows and starts staking its claim on areas you normally enjoy looking at. As Harm OCD worsens, your fear of knives, for example, becomes a fear of cooking, and then a fear of the kitchen, and then not even wanting to think about food. You have to be willing to wander through some of those darker, scarier territories, not to live there but to step on the weeds enough so they don't grow into the rest of your mental landscape.

Mindfulness works by repeatedly repositioning you as an observer behind the flashlight instead of as a victim of what the flashlight shines on. Consider the difference between "I am going to cause harm" and "I am noticing thoughts about causing harm." Consider the difference between "I am freaking out" and "I am aware of the presence of anxiety." By shifting your perspective, you can stay present with whatever the OCD dishes out. Rather than fighting the OCD with ineffective compulsions, you fight it with the one thing OCD cannot counter—willingness to experience things as they are.

A Brief Mindfulness Meditation

1. +Find a comfortable, mostly quiet place to sit.

2. Close your eyes and put your attention on the weight of your body against the chair or floor. Notice any other senses that may be active, such as hearing or smelling. Think: *This is me in this moment.*

3. Direct your attention to the sensation of breathing. This will be your anchor. I like to rest my attention on the sensation of my stomach pressing on my shirt as I inhale, but

you can attend to wherever the breath is most easy to recognize for you.

4. The name of the game is to leave your attention here. It's
    not about trying to focus hard on the breath, but rather
    resting your attention here like you might rest your head on
    a loved one's belly. (I use my dog's belly as a pillow some-
    times.) Watch the breath begin, the body expand, the
    breath shift from inhale to exhale, the breath leave, and
    the breath shift again from exhale back to inhale.

5. As you continue to do this, you will have thoughts. They
    will range anywhere from thoughts about how boring or
    awkward meditation can be to the scary thoughts your
    OCD is always going on about. This is fine. Actually, it's
    what the meditation is for. When you become aware that
    you are *attending* to your thoughts, simply acknowledge
    that you are thinking and return to your breath. Set a
    timer and try this for five minutes.

Don't worry if all you got was five minutes of having thoughts hit
you in the head. The question is, were you mindful of the experience?
Did you attempt to be more aware of *where* your mind was in each
moment? If you caught yourself swimming around in the thoughts and
feelings, trying to change them, and then you gently placed yourself
back on the other side of the glass even once, then you were practicing
mindfulness.

Self-Compassion and Harm OCD

People with OCD often have a very loud self-critical voice inside.
People with Harm OCD probably get the worst of it. It starts with the
unwanted thoughts themselves—ugly, vicious, unyielding, and presented without context or any trigger warnings or disclaimers. But
then the voice that follows may be even worse. *You're disgusting. You're
a horrible person. You shouldn't have had that thought. What's wrong with*

you? Who thinks that way? You are a bad person. You are the worst person.
Guilt for having harm thoughts and a pervasive black cloud of self-hatred often follow. This voice is also a product of the OCD, but because it sounds like you, it stings all the more. The voice may continue to taunt you, positing that since only a horrible person has these thoughts, you are somehow more susceptible to doing the things that only horrible people do, despite the fact that there is no evidence that people with OCD act on their unwanted thoughts.

For many with Harm OCD, this results in such a profound mistrust of the self that basic daily activities feel too risky. *How can I justify spending time with my children if I could pitch them over the second-floor railing at any time? Who am I to hold this pen if I could stab the person next to me at any moment? Why should I be allowed to watch the news if a story about a murderer could send me into a psychopathic rage against my neighbors? Who am I to pet this dog when I can't be sure I won't strangle him?*

In treating OCD, we work on confronting our fears and changing the behaviors that fuel them. But we often forget to work on challenging how we talk to ourselves about having the fears in the first place. If the OCD can effectively cut you down as a human being for even *having* the thought, how will you find the strength to fight your OCD? Compassion researcher Kristin Neff identifies compassion as a combination of empathy (the ability to feel what others are feeling) and the desire to ease suffering (Neff 2011). Self-compassion is thus applying this concept to oneself the way we might intuitively apply it to others in pain. If we understand how to access self-compassion, we can use this as an effective tool against OCD. Ask yourself how often you do compulsions just because you fear that you will treat yourself badly if you don't do them. What if you didn't have to be afraid of that because you knew that no matter what happens, you'll help *you* get through it?

Being Honest About Your Experience

Neff describes three core elements of self-compassion: mindfulness, common humanity, and self-kindness. Each of these elements can highlight how self-compassion is also about being *honest* about your experience of having Harm OCD. The OCD lies all day about what a terrible person you are and it does this to wear you down and get you to do compulsions. Honesty about your experience is a great weapon in your arsenal against the OCD. "I am a horrible excuse for a human being and if people knew what I thought, they'd want to lock me up" is not an honest statement. It's a fear. An honest statement is "I have unwanted harm thoughts and I worry that they mean something bad about me." This is also a *mindful* statement. Remember, mindfulness is observing an experience without judgment in the present moment. It's viewing things as they *are*, not as your OCD says they might be.

"Common humanity" refers to the recognition that your experiences are shared by others, whether the OCD wants you to think so or not. Many people (including those without OCD) have unwanted taboo intrusive thoughts (Rachman and de Silva 1978). Compare the dishonest statement of "I am a freak for having these thoughts" to "Many people have unwanted thoughts, and people like me with OCD are especially likely to notice and worry about them." This is important to acknowledge because the likelihood is that if you did not have OCD, these same thoughts with violent content would be viewed as nothing but random pieces of mental debris. Part of being self-compassionate is taking an extra moment to remind yourself both that we all have violent thoughts and *also* that you are not alone as an OCD sufferer concerned about them.

"Self-kindness" simply means treating yourself as you would treat anyone else you cared about who was suffering. Self-criticism focuses on everything you think you are doing wrong. But if you are reading this book, you have to admit that you are doing at least *something* right in your battle with unwanted harm thoughts. You picked up a self-help book. See the difference between the dishonest and self-critical statement of "I'm such a disgusting loser for having these thoughts" and the more honest and kind statement: "This is so hard, but I'm doing the best I can to resist compulsions right now and trying to learn what I can to get control over my Harm OCD."

These three concepts can be put together into a coping statement or they can be used à la carte, but cultivating an internal voice that is honest instead of self-abusive, that wants you to win the battle against Harm OCD, is a wise move. I'll give you some tips on creating self-compassion statements for your specific obsessions in part 2.

H.E.A.L.ing from Harm OCD

In this chapter, we have looked at four approaches to reclaiming power over your Harm OCD, namely: cognitive approaches, exposure and response prevention, mindfulness, and self-compassion. The opposite of Harm is HEAL, so let's use this as an acronym for your four main Harm OCD-fighting tools.

H: Have Another Look (cognitive approaches). This is really all that cognitive approaches to OCD require—that you have another look at your thoughts before doing compulsions. Noting cognitive distortions and weighing them against other potential ways of thinking about an experience requires you only to step back and recognize, "Hey, I'm thinking and there is a *way* in which I am thinking right now that may or may not be useful."

E: Exposure and Response Prevention (ERP). Getting out in front of a trigger and learning how to be in its presence intentionally and without compulsions is the most effective way to break free from the obsessive-compulsive cycle and put an end to the negative reinforcement that keeps you stuck. How can you lean in to an OCD punch and use the energy this produces to come out on top of your fear? By engaging in exposures to the violent thoughts while reducing safety behaviors and eliminating compulsions, you can change the hold this disorder has over you.

A: Acceptance and Mindfulness. Everything you need to know about mindfulness can be summed up in the words, "Hey, look at that." By stepping back and recognizing that you are experiencing thoughts, feelings, and sensations, not threats, warnings, and condemnations, you can find stillness and openness to whatever your mind happens to be offering. By accepting the presence of these unwanted thoughts, you disempower them. Remember, by developing your mindfulness skills, you can stop viewing your harm thoughts as sharks with you in a shark tank and instead view your thoughts as sharks with you at an aquarium, simply swimming by.

L: Love Yourself (self-compassion). Self-compassion means treating yourself as you would your best friend. If you accept the presence of your thoughts (not the meaning or content of your thoughts), recognize that you are not alone in your frustration and fear, and focus on what you're doing right and how you can help yourself, the sadistic voice of OCD doesn't stand a chance. These tenets of mindfulness, common humanity, and self-kindness combine to bring your attention away from self-doubt and toward your profound personal strengths.

It's important to remember that these are not separate approaches in the sense that they should be implemented in any particular order, or that any one approach is always going to be more effective than another. In fact, *all* of the elements of HEAL will include all of the *other* elements of HEAL. Having another look (H) at your experience by recognizing distorted thinking requires you to stay exposed to the thoughts (E). This requires that you first accept (A) that these are the thoughts going through your head and finally, by choosing to respond differently to your OCD and being willing to accept uncertainty in that moment, you are engaging in self-compassion, and treating yourself as someone worthy of love (L).

You're Not Crazy

So far you've done a lot of exposure. You picked up a book with the words "Harm OCD" in the title. You read the first chapter that went over assessment and diagnosis, and that probably triggered you to no end with commentary on all the problems you might have besides Harm OCD. Yet you persevered. You moved on to read about why we have these thoughts and how we can never be certain about them because we can't be certain of anything. This might have been upsetting too, yet you persevered. You read through a crash course of treatment tools, many of which may seem daunting or too hard right now. Your OCD is always trying to make you feel like you're different from others, and in some ways you do have to be different. To stand up to Harm OCD, you have to possess a quality of bravery that not everyone possesses. You're not crazy. You're something far more interesting.

Recap

Okay, chapter 2 and all of part 1 of this book are behind you. Well done! Chapter 2 reviewed a lot of clinical material at once, so don't worry if you feel like you don't have a firm grasp on all the concepts. They will each be explored in more depth in part 2, where we look at different manifestations of Harm OCD. What were some of the basic ideas? First, at the core of mastery over OCD is your willingness to accept uncertainty. Though your Harm OCD presents you with terrifying thought content, uncertainty remains a constant. But accepting uncertainty doesn't mean you have to resign yourself to being unhappy or to lie to yourself about the odds of your fears being true. Next we looked at four main tools for fighting Harm OCD, which you can remember with the acronym H.E.A.L. *H* stands for Have Another Look, which refers to cognitive approaches that can help you challenge distorted thinking that fuels your OCD. *E* stands for ERP (exposure and response prevention), which means learning to stop doing compulsions by challenging yourself to confront your fears methodically. *A* stands for acceptance, which is an important part of mindfulness, the ability to observe your thoughts and feeling as they are in the present moment. L stands for Love Yourself, referring to using self-compassion to break away from the cycle of self-hatred that OCD uses to keep you enslaved. In the chapters ahead, I will take these treatment tools and techniques and apply them to four specific manifestations of Harm OCD.

PART 2

Using the Principles of H.E.A.L. for Different Manifestations of Harm OCD

The next four chapters are going to cover four common manifestations of Harm OCD. You may find that only one resonates with you or you may find that a few or all of them do. It is not unusual for Harm OCD to bounce around. You might think of OCD as a carnivorous dinosaur from *Jurassic Park*, constantly testing the fences for weaknesses to see a way through to wreaking havoc. The OCD lives off of compulsions, so it will look for whatever is most likely to get you to respond compulsively. This is why establishing broad OCD-fighting, uncertainty-accepting skills is more effective than arguing in your head over the content of any individual thought. The first chapter of this section will focus on this fear at the identity level, as well as the fear of causing harm through lack of vigilance or error. I recommend that you read this chapter first to lay the groundwork for the following three chapters on the fear of impulsive harm, the fear of self-harm, and the fear of harming your children.

CHAPTER 3

Fear of a Harmful Identity

At the beginning of this book, I introduced you to Joanna, who feared that her lack of vigilance could have put her husband at unnecessary risk of poison. In that example, she also worried that she might have harbored unwanted bad intentions. She wanted certainty that she was careful enough not to cause accidental harm and moral enough not to cause intentional harm. You may have noticed how *careful* and *moral* can feel like the same thing. Like many people who struggle with this kind of OCD, Joanna was faced with an impossible task—to become certain about what her intentions *were*. But we can only know what our intentions *are* in the present moment.

People with Harm OCD have a tendency to attach distorted meanings to their intrusive thoughts, specifically believing that the thoughts must mean they are "bad" or "dangerous" people, and this causes so much distress that it makes them respond with more extreme attempts (compulsions) to neutralize the thoughts (Riskind, Ayers, and Wright 2007). I don't think words can do justice to the level of suffering people with OCD endure when they come to the false conclusion that their violent thoughts make them vile people. I say you're not violent *or* vile. You're just too tuned in to a scary station in your head and you've yet to establish the skill set required to permit yourself to tune in to other stations.

Fearing Unintentional Harm Through Lack of Vigilance

The majority of this book focuses on the fear of *intending* to cause harm, the fear of committing acts of violence, or the burden of thinking violent thoughts. The term "Harm OCD" is rarely used in the clinical literature. Research tends to look at "violent" or "aggressive" obsessions. Yet, if I leave a knife on the table and my little daughter cuts herself with it by accident, I am going to feel pretty bad about it. I'm going to think that I should have taken more care to make sure she wouldn't come in harm's way. I might wonder: How much effort should I put into keeping harm from reaching her? If I admit the truth, that no matter how much the effort I make, it is still limited, I am left vulnerable to attacks from the OCD saying that I am a harmful person. This can be viewed as Harm OCD too, whether it involves the presence of violent thoughts or not.

When school is in session, I help get my kids ready in the morning and I wait with them for the bus at the bottom of the driveway. I spend as much time as I can protecting them, teaching them, entertaining them, and letting them know that they are loved. When the bus comes, I put them on it and I go to work. That's right, I devote all of my energy to keeping them safe and then I put them on a bus, driven by a man I don't know, to a location I won't be at. What if this bus driver decides today's the day he wants to start drinking first thing in the morning and he passes out at the wheel and sends the bus flying into oncoming traffic, killing several people, including my children? Okay, that would be tragic, but why did I let them on the bus in the first place? I could have driven them to school. I could have gotten to work late. The answer is, I limited the amount of effort toward keeping them safe to something I felt was reasonable. But how do I know for certain that it *was* reasonable and not evidence of a lack of feeling, lack of compassion, or lack of grip on reality? I don't. I have to be able to *not-know*. If you are unable to sit with not-knowing, the OCD can convince you of pretty much anything, and *that* can keep you from doing anything you really value. Knowing things (for example, being confident that my children are safe on the bus) and not-knowing things (for example, being able to go to work without being certain of their status) are both important skills.

Obsessing About Being Good

Living with OCD is very much like having a voice in your head that repeatedly admonishes you for being a bad person. Escaping such self-abuse is one reason you do compulsions. OCD says you're bad because of things you've done, things you've thought, and even things you haven't done or thought but could have! So how do you accept uncertainty about being "bad"? If I treat my violent thoughts as just OCD chatter, I have to accept the possibility that they could be something more. If I accept the possibility that I may be wrong about OCD, that these thoughts may actually *be* dangerous signs or something like that, then how can I morally let them go? Shouldn't I devote 100% of my energy and attention to making sure my potential sociopathic traits don't go unchecked? Should there even be a limit to the amount of effort I put into making sure I am not a bad person? If I ever do hurt someone, the horror of that won't just be about the act itself, but about the fact that I was not vigilant enough to prevent it early on when I knew I had bad thoughts! Quite a mess.

The reason why you suffer so pervasively with the fear of being a harmful or "bad" person has to do in part with how you set your standards in the first place. People with OCD set the standard for good in terms of certainty. In other words, *I am good when I am certain I am good. I am bad when I am uncertain.* People without OCD may or may not set their standards for "goodness" high, but they set them mostly in some achievable place. They either achieve it and feel content or they don't and they feel guilty. People with OCD cannot achieve their standard for goodness because the standard is *certainty* and *certainty doesn't exist.* So no matter how hard you try, you end up feeling guilty anyway, thinking you're getting close at times, but never quite getting there. Why? Because "there" is an illusion created by your OCD. In other words, many people have what you might call unrealistic expectations for determining whether or not they are good people who have done no harm. They work harder than they have to in order to feel good about themselves. But OCD sufferers don't just have unrealistic expectations—they have *unreal* expectations.

Assessing for Safety

Assessing simply means asking the right questions to help find out more about something and, with the right information, identifying a course of action that is most likely to be helpful. Assessing whether you are an inherently harmful or immoral person is challenging because some of the more obvious answers turn out to be messy when you look closely. For example, *Do you like harm thoughts?* Naturally, you'd assume that not liking harm thoughts is a good answer because it suggests you just have OCD and don't need to worry about the rest of it. But what if you like *some* harm thoughts sometimes? Doesn't this book repeatedly say it's normal to have these thoughts? If they're normal, why not like them if you can? So the questions for assessing when it might be appropriate to be concerned have to be more specific and focused. Some important questions could be:

- Do you voluntarily fantasize for large amounts of time about your violent thoughts coming true?

- Do you wish you could get away with acting out on your violent thoughts?

- How would you *feel* about these events coming true?

- How would you feel about the way your actions would affect others?

Proper assessment by a mental health professional may tease out useful differences between someone whose main issues involve being overly afraid of unwanted thoughts and someone with, say, poor anger-management skills or a lack of empathy. Sociopathy (a word used synonymously with Antisocial Personality Disorder) is characterized by an indifference for, or lack of guilt regarding, the suffering of others (APA 2013). Of course, as you read this, your OCD is likely to tell you that you have to check and make sure that you feel *enough* guilt about this or that idea. That's not the point. We have to accept uncertainty in all things. But in treatment, the therapist needs enough information to determine when exposure therapy is going to be effective and when some other treatment for some other issue makes more sense.

All this being said, consider that it is your very interest in the subject of being good that points to the likelihood that you are not a sociopath. More likely, your OCD makes you overflowing with empathy and compassion. This overflow is actually the root of the problem.

Common Obsessions in Fearing a Harmful Identity

- Fear of hitting someone with the car and not knowing it (or knew it but blocked it out mentally)

- Fear of inadvertently influencing someone to do harm

- Fear of facilitating harm to come to your loved ones (or pets) by lack of vigilance

- Fear of worsening someone's life as a form of harm

- Fear of causing harm by spreading contaminants due to not washing thoroughly or not avoiding vigilantly

- Fear of allowing others to be harmed by leaving contaminated items accessible

- Fear of poisoning others with expired food, "unsafe" food, or improperly cooked food, or by allowing contaminants to have touched food

- Fear of being in denial of a latent other-sexuality (gay if you identify as straight, straight if you identify as gay, and so on), resulting in severe emotional harm to a significant other

- Fear of causing harm to others by negligence (for example, causing a fire by not checking if the stove is off, causing a burglary by not checking if the doors are locked)

- Fear of allowing harm to occur by leaving "dangerous" objects around (for example, seeing a potentially distracting object in the street that could cause a traffic accident or seeing a loose nail that could be used as a weapon or cause a structure to collapse)

- Fear of causing a romantic partner such distress that that partner might harm him- or herself or have an unhappy or "wasted" life

- Fear of harming loved ones by not perfectly meeting their needs (for example, harming a child by not playing enough with her and making her feel "abandoned")

- Fear of harming loved ones by exposing them to "inappropriate" material (for example, violent movies or age-inappropriate music)

- Fear of harming someone by saying the wrong thing or getting someone in trouble inadvertently (for example, getting your coworker fired or causing your therapist to have her license revoked)

- Fear of contributing to global problems that cause harm to innocent people (for example, buying an article of clothing that might have been manufactured in poor conditions where children are harmed)

This may seem like a long list, but it's really just a list of things I have heard in my clinical practice. Your unique ability to access the creative mind likely has you already noticing other examples I've missed. If there's a way for harm to come to you or others and for it be your fault, you'll think of it eventually!

Common Compulsions for the Fear of a Harmful Identity

This whole book could be filled with a list of compulsions people do when they fear living with a harmful identity. This is by no means a comprehensive list, but a small sample of behaviors you might find yourself doing in response to unwanted violent thoughts or moral concerns about doing harm:

- Mentally reviewing past acts, conversations, or thoughts to assess if there were any signs of violent or sociopathic behavior

- Mental rituals that include trying to figure out with certainty if you did, could, or would commit a harmful act

- Researching serial killers for reassurance to determine if there are important similarities in personality or behavior

- Testing your mind to see if you like harmful thoughts

- Avoiding triggers in the media, news stories, and so on

- Avoiding situations or objects where unintentional harm could take place (for example, driving, cooking, using chemicals)

- Avoiding situations where there is any responsibility for protecting others from harm (for example, babysitting or visiting someone in the hospital)

- Avoiding emotional states you imagine could lead to harm (for example, anger, stress, lack of control)

- Neutralizing violent thoughts with "clean" or "safe" thoughts

- Excessive checking of self or others to ensure no harm was done

- Excessive checking of locks, faucets, outlets, and so on where you imagine harm could occur

- Seeking reassurance from others that you are a good person and not a sociopath, and that you would never harm someone

- Confessing perceived bad thoughts or acts

Let's take a closer look at how the OCD can get you stuck in this kind of mind trap and how you can get yourself unstuck using the tools of HEAL.

H: Have Another Look

Cognitive approaches to the fear of a harmful or immoral identity can be very useful. If you can see how your way of processing the harm thoughts is pushing you into compulsions, you can shift your approach to something more objective and rational. This doesn't mean reassuring yourself that you're good. A client who was frustrated with his OCD always telling him he's bad once asked me why OCD doesn't try to convince him that he's good. The answer is because that doesn't take convincing.

A good way of understanding this part of treating OCD is to imagine the OCD as having its own wants and needs. By using cognitive distortions, it shows you what it *wants* you to think. Let's take a look at how some of the cognitive distortions common in OCD can present themselves in this specific manifestation:

Thought-Action Fusion: *Allowing these harm thoughts to persist is causing harm to others.* This is a common and scary cognitive error, but the fact that it is scary shouldn't change the fabric of reality. Whether you worry that your thoughts will cause a harmful outcome or you worry that your thoughts are themselves immoral acts, remember that what happens in your mind actually stays in your mind.

Catastrophizing: *I am going to live in misery and denial if I can't prove that my intentions were good.* The surest way to bully you into doing compulsions is to threaten a lifetime of unhappiness and to convince you of the lie that doing compulsions will protect you from such a life. Since you can't predict the future, trying to protect yourself from it with mental rituals is a poor use of your attention. Not only can you not predict the future, you can never be certain what your intentions *were* in the past. We only ever know what our intentions are right now in this exact moment.

Discounting the Positive: *This thought proves I am a monster.* Yeah, but what about all the people you *haven't* killed in your mind today? The OCD doesn't want you to recognize the lifetime of compassionate behavior and love you've displayed up to five seconds ago. It wants you to focus only on this one thought in this moment as indicating who you are.

Tunnel Vision: *I responded to that article about a murderer the way I did because I am like that.* It's important to remember that you notice what you notice because that's what obsessing about something means. If you have a fear of being a dangerous person and you notice your heart rate go up when you read about a school shooting, then it is wise to acknowledge that this is a predictable reaction and not a sign or premonition.

Emotional Reasoning: *I feel like a monster.* Treating your feelings like completely reliable sources of information about who you are can easily backfire. Sometimes you are terrified of your thoughts, and sometimes you are bored by those same thoughts.

Shoulds: *I should never have violent thoughts.* Here, you need to pay attention to the role of unreal expectations discussed earlier. Violent thoughts are a necessary and useful part of the human psyche. You could argue that it would benefit you not to spend a ton of time dwelling on violent thoughts, and that your attention may have more valuable places to rest. This is not the same thing as rigidly demanding that you never have these thoughts.

E: Exposure and Response Prevention

For instructions on how to methodically construct an ERP plan, I recommend working with a therapist who specializes in OCD. If you are unable to access one, then there are several excellent self-help workbooks on OCD that can go into greater specifics on constructing an ERP treatment plan (see https://iocdf.org/books/ for a comprehensive list). Here I will go over some useful ideas to consider for doing exposure to your fear of a harmful identity. First, let's review the three rules about doing ERP from chapter 2.

Important Rules for ERP

- **Don't do exposure in a manner where accidental harm is likely to take place.** Exposure to fears of a harmful identity can be nuanced, and the line between being less compulsive and being dangerous to others is not always clear. Leaving a door ajar when your OCD tells you that someone could bump into it and hurt their head could be an effective exposure. Pulling a parking brake one time instead of three and accepting that it might malfunction and cause your car to roll into traffic might be good. Placing a bunch of broken glass and marbles on a stair case, not so much. Always bear in mind that the goal is to learn to live with uncertainty. This does not mean you have to try to create chaos or actively bring harm to others.

- **You don't have to violate your values in the name of ERP.** I shed no tears for ants when I willfully step on or poison them. If my OCD told me that this meant I was a closeted sociopath, then it might be a good exposure to step on ants when I see them and even diabolically laugh to myself about it. But if intentionally killing a living creature goes against your morals (or your religious faith), then it is not the best direction to take ERP. Some religious practices set rules for types of thoughts you are allowed to dwell on. Though most educated clergy will recommend prioritizing your mental health over sticking to the letter of a religious law, you may wish to consult with an advisor on what kind of exposures to uncertainty can be effective without directly going against your religious beliefs. In any case, challenging yourself to accept uncertainty about "right" and "wrong" doesn't mean you have to cheat, steal, or violate the rights of others.

- **No testing.** Whatever you do to get out in front of your fears and master your Harm OCD, you must take care not to allow exposures to become checking compulsions. If you watch a movie about a serial killer and spend the whole time analyzing whether you are or are not too much like that character, then you are not really doing exposure, but are just testing your reactions. Exposure and response prevention includes preventing the attempts to get certainty about whatever reactions the exposure brings about.

In Vivo Exposure Tips

- Visiting people or places that trigger your unwanted thoughts (and accepting or agreeing with them as they arise)

- Watching triggering movies or shows about harmful people or with violent imagery (remember, don't use this to self-reassure, but to practice being triggered without compulsions)

- Reduce or eliminate unnecessary safety behaviors (for example, excessive washing to avoid spreading harmful contaminants)

- Reduce or eliminate unnecessary checking (for example, checking rearview mirror to make sure you didn't hit someone)

Consider, what would a person do who did not care as much or mind as much about caring? How can I do exposure to the idea that I may not care the most? The goal is not to care less but to actually be more effective in choosing behaviors that are in line with your values. Devoting your life to attending to moral perfection is not likely part of your value system. If you have Harm OCD, your moral compass may be bent in a perfectionist direction. This means that when you do exposure, you are going to *feel* less moral in the moment, but you are probably still landing somewhere on the decent side of moral behavior. ERP enables you to readjust the compass by retraining yourself to behave noncompulsively. Compulsions always strengthen the OCD, which always takes you further away from your loved ones, your goals, and your potentials.

Acceptance and Motivation Scripts

Confronting the idea that there is a limit to how much you care about keeping others safe requires some real courage. An acceptance and motivation script might help point you in the right direction. Recall from part 1, here you want to try to honestly answer four questions about your fear and what you plan to do about it. Start by writing about how you are going to do exposure, or what safety behaviors or avoidances you are going to give up. Then describe what it is you think this really risks. Use detail as best you can. Face it—if you are planning to slack off even in the slightest regard (according to your OCD), you are opening a doorway to potential harm to others, no matter how indirectly. What does it look like if the less vigilant version of yourself meets feared outcomes? Then go on to describe what is likely to happen if you continue to obey your OCD and live submissively under its iron fist. How much checking and avoiding and reassurance seeking will you engage in if OCD has its way? What are the real-life consequences of this and how tolerable are they? Lastly, consider what it really means to you to be a "good" person (and not just technically certain you are right). How does this conceptualization of your own goodness conflict with OCD's demands? Here you should answer the question of why you are willing to take the risk and do exposure.

An Example of an Acceptance and Motivation Script: "I am going to start barbecuing in the back yard and will limit my checking of the propane tank to one time only. This may result in me leaving it on somehow and later causing an explosion that sets fire to my house and kills my family. I may realize that this happened because I was not vigilant enough and I may spend the rest of my life mired in regret. But if I continue to avoid using the grill, I will continue to foster resentment from my children and further strengthen my OCD to the point where I can't use anything that involves fire. I'll devote huge portions of my life to checking and I still won't get a guarantee of no harm. I want to be the kind of parent who grills hamburgers and celebrates outdoors with his family. I believe that a good father is a present father and even though there are so many things that I can mess up, it's still worth it for me to take the risk of standing up to my OCD."

Flooding Scripts

In this form of scripting, you are trying to generate the emotional world in which you are most aware of the urge to do compulsions. In the context of fearing a more general "harmfulness," these compulsions might be simply to self-reassure that you are good and to distinguish yourself from some kind of "bad" person. Again, it's important not to let these types of scripts devolve into a sort of compulsive self-punishment exercise. Yes, you are trying to generate bad feelings so you can be better at being in their presence without compulsions, but you are not trying to criticize or condemn yourself. If you find that a flooding script produces fear or self-doubt, then you are probably on the right track. But if the script simply makes you feel more convinced of your fears and more depressed about the likelihood of them coming true, then you are probably engaging in compulsive self-punishment. This is important to pay attention to because the use of self-punishment as a thought-control strategy actually makes you *more* compulsive because it strengthens your false beliefs about the importance of controlling these thoughts (Jacoby et al. 2016).

One way to approach this style of scripting is to consider what all of your cognitive distortions are and try to write them with the distortions intact. In other words, use this exercise to catastrophize, magnify, and emotionally reason your way into the fear (but as always, without compulsions). Remember, it's not important for a flooding script to make any real sense chronologically or narratively. As long as it puts you in the emotional space with the OCD and gives you a chance to stand there without compulsions, then it can help break the cycle.

An Example of a Flooding Script: "These thoughts will continue to pervade my mind and eventually wear me down to become a person who does not care who lives or dies. I may start hitting people with the car, but won't care. Or maybe I'll feed someone poison just to see how it affects them. If I never get caught doing these immoral acts, I will just live with the

knowledge that I am not really who I say I am. I am an impos-
ter pretending to be a normal human, but in secret willingly
going out of my way to let bad things happen to good people,
to strangers. If I see a piece of broken glass on the street, I will
leave it there and let someone step on it and get cut. Maybe
someone will pick it up and use it to cut someone else. I don't
care. I will allow these things to happen and rationalize that I
can't control everything, but deep down I will know that I am
simply thriving on making the world a darker place. I will
become comfortable with people getting hurt and will make a
negative contribution to humanity. I will like my violent
thoughts and I will let them define me. At some point I may
rationalize killing someone. I might get caught and put in a
mental institution or executed."

A: Acceptance and Mindfulness

You are not the greatest person who ever lived. (You probably didn't
expect to hear something like that in a self-help book! But hear me
out.) You may be great, but you're human and you do have your flaws.
Some of these are regular everyday flaws we grapple with and strive to
overcome. Some of these aren't flaws at all but just thoughts about
being flawed. When your mind is constantly telling you that you're
basically good on the outside but a monster on the inside, your best bet
is to learn to be able to view the whole self by developing your mindfulness skills.

You have thoughts about not having done enough to protect yourself and others from your inherent horribleness. We can say those
thoughts come from your OCD, that they are meaningless, and that
you can ignore them. But we can only say that once we accept that
these are the thoughts that are going through your head. Mindfulness
allows you to position yourself as an observer of these thoughts, not a
judge of them. OCD wants you in full-time judge mode. Learning to be
a nonjudgmental observer, then, is your ultimate weapon against OCD.

In meditation, we want to strengthen our ability to observe where the mind goes when we lighten our grip on it. If you worry about harboring a harmful identity or harming others due to irresponsibility, you may notice that a lot of the thoughts that crop up in meditation have to do with real and imagined mistakes from your past. You may also notice passing feelings of guilt or shame. Try to view these as mere objects of attention instead of as projects to work on or resolve. The better student you are of what arises in the mind, the less power your OCD has over you.

L: Love Yourself

There's nothing wrong with wanting to know what kind of person you are and yearning for that to be a "good" person. The problem with OCD is that it has a way of making you feel unsafe in your positive assumptions about yourself. It demands constant attention and constant evidence that you are good and not bad. It points out every unscrupulous thought, every moment of indifference, and says, "Cling more tightly to your identity before you lose it!" The more you cling to the identity, the more it feels like it could slip through your fingers.

To make matters worse, punishment thought-control strategies (that is, beating yourself up and blaming yourself) are significantly associated with "unacceptable" thoughts and thoughts about responsibility for harm (Lee et al. 2016). The more "unacceptable" thoughts you have, the more you are inclined to treat yourself badly, the more you believe the OCD nonsense, and the less uncertainty you are willing to tolerate. Learning to love yourself as a person who has harm thoughts starts with mindful acceptance. *These are the thoughts going through my head and that's just what is.*

Now consider that everyone has these thoughts and everyone struggles with them from time to time, but people with OCD are wired to struggle with them more. Instead of framing yourself as sick or defective, view yourself as embodying a trait that is shared by many other people. Don't let the OCD trick you into isolating yourself from humanity. Remember that you are running equipment in your head that takes some special nuance to operate smoothly and you may need to give yourself credit and additional support for standing up to the OCD. Using these concepts, it's always a good idea to reframe your self-hating assessments of life with Harm OCD into self-compassionate statements. Remember, they are more honest.

An Example of a Coping Statement: "I'm feeling afraid that I could have harmed someone and I'm disgusted with myself for thinking about these things. Nobody likes feeling doubtful about who they are and we all have unpleasant thoughts to contend with sometimes. I'm doing a pretty good job keeping an open mind about this being OCD even while I fear it means something terrible. I'm going to give myself permission to be uncertain about this right now and to resist compulsions. I can invite myself to do one of my exposure exercises and remember that this is a process that is challenging."

You're Not Crazy

People probably underestimate how seriously you want to do no harm. If they don't suffer from OCD the way you do, it's impossible to imagine what it's like to stay as committed as you are to guaranteeing no harm to others. The OCD tries to corner you between a rock and a hard place. *Care about everything 100% or resign yourself to being a monster who doesn't care about anyone or anything. Then prove that the caring you're doing is genuine!* This includes caring 100% (or not) about your own happiness or fulfillment with a mind full of violent or repugnant images. Well, it can't be done and it shouldn't be done. OCD accuses you of being inhuman, but then charges you with the task of being superhuman? Now *that* is a crazy idea.

Recap

H: Have Another Look. The way we think about our thoughts and feelings affects the way we consider doing or resisting compulsions. Jumping to conclusions that this or that must mean you are a closeted sociopath makes it easy for OCD to dominate the conversation. Recognize when your thinking is distorted without reassuring yourself. Acknowledge what you don't know, that you can't predict the future, and that you can't be too rigid about what happens in your mind. It can make the difference between fueling OCD or defeating OCD at its own game.

E: Exposure and Response Prevention. By getting out ahead of the OCD and choosing to be exposed to things that require you to confront uncertainty, you can become a pro at resisting compulsions. You can confront your fear by letting go of unnecessary safety behaviors and committing to do things and be around people even when they trigger you. Scripting about the idea that you could be harboring a malevolent identity can be an especially effective way to get at this kind of Harm OCD.

A: Acceptance and Mindfulness. The human mind can be trained to walk a path, but not a perfectly straight one. Like a puppy, it can't help but sniff around new territory and present you with ideas that may be confusing or upsetting, or that may appear threatening. Remembering that thoughts and feelings are always simple objects of attention can make the decision to resist compulsions much easier to access.

L: Love and Self-Compassion. You care too much because you think too much because you care too much. People with Harm OCD who worry about harboring a harmful identity or who worry about grotesque thoughts interfering with joyfulness are people who are sensitive to the human condition. Learning to be grateful that you are creative and compassionate and understanding that this combo sometimes leads to you meandering into scary philosophical territory can release you from the contract of self-criticism. It is in this state that we do our best against the OCD.

CHAPTER 4

Fear of Harming Others

Most people do not spend their every waking moment worried about exploding outward and destroying things in their path. It's as if they know that any impulses to act out in violent chaos will be automatically suppressed. In fact, they may be so suppressed that they don't even think they experience the impulses at all! (I occasionally encounter people who claim they never think of turning their car into oncoming traffic, but these people seem really peculiar to me.) What would it be like not to have that resting sense of safety, not to have that confidence at all? What would it be like to feel impulses that are anathema to your wishes and at the same time feel absolutely no safety net besides sheer will? If you're reading this, you may already know.

Near the beginning of this book, I gave the example of Mandy, whose Harm OCD started after learning about a violent crime. The thoughts bounced around in her head starting with *Why would someone do that?* to *Would I ever do that?* to *What's to stop me from doing that?* Her compulsions ranged from mental rituals aimed at proving that she would never act out, to avoiding triggers that made her think about acting out, to seeking reassurance from various sources that she would not act out. What was worse, when the obsession was at its most intense, she could swear she felt a sensation in her hands that suggested she was about to act out physically. This made being within reaching distance of another person incredibly frightening. Sometimes she would sit on her hands, just to feel more certain that she couldn't use them for harm. Her daily life became a sort of booby-trapped journey where every step along the way could be the step right before doing something terrible. She also had to keep this a secret from everyone she cared about. If they ever knew about the ticking time bomb she believed herself to be, she imagined they could never love or trust her again.

There are a couple of different ways to look at this fear of loss of control and impulsive harm. One theory suggests that these thoughts are normal responses when people are provoked or their goals are obstructed—that these experiences trigger aggressive fantasies but that people without OCD usually just disregard them. The trigger could be something small, like learning you have to go to a work meeting you'd rather avoid, but nonetheless it still produces these meaningless violent thoughts (Riskind, Ayers, and Wright 2007). When people with OCD become aware of these types of thoughts, they interpret them as "motivated intentions" and then they feel they have to be certain that they are under control (Aardema and O'Connor 2007). Think of the times you wondered, *Did that thought mean I wanted to do that horrible thing?* This leads to compulsive efforts to be certain you won't harm anyone, which leads to worsened obsessions. It's important to understand that this does not mean you are a more violent person. It means you are just more likely to become aware of naturally arising violent thoughts than the average person.

Another theory suggests that, unlike contamination fears, these types of Harm OCD fears are just autogenous, meaning they simply pop into your head and bother you whether prompted by external events or not (Lee and Kwon 2003). You get bothered by their *presence*, as opposed to them being present because you became bothered. While these theories continue to be explored, it's useful to remember that understanding *why* the thoughts are there still doesn't relieve you of the actual problem of how to handle them in the present moment. The OCD will often keep you focused on the task of trying to prove the reason the thoughts are there, but this is a distraction from the only project that will really help you overcome the disorder—accepting uncertainty.

Assessing for Safety

What will make me certain I will not engage in a violent act against another person? This is a trick question because it asks for something that doesn't actually exist: *certainty*. We cannot know if or when we will do something impulsively because, by definition, we can only know when an impulse is being responded to, not before the impulse occurs. That being said, there are some specific questions worth exploring with a mental health professional to assess for safety when it comes to intrusive thoughts about acting out violently:

- Do you have a history of engaging in violent acts? No, I'm not talking about the time when you were a kid and you punched your brother for breaking your favorite toy, or that time you tugged on the dog's leash a little aggressively when he wouldn't obey your commands. Rather, do you have a historical pattern of resolving your differences through acts of violence?

- Do your violent thoughts seem completely reasonable or, rather, do they seem to conflict with your overall desires and sense of self?

- Are you developing a plan to harm another person in a specific way at a specific time? Mental healthcare providers in the US are bound by laws stating that they have a duty to warn potential victims and call the police if they believe a patient is going to harm another person.

Golden and colleagues (2016) provide a case conceptualization of a woman with fears of harming her husband. In addition to assessing her for homicidal ideation with questions like those above, they also collected information from family members who could objectively verify what she claimed. Because OCD thrives on pairing the worst things you can think of with the people you care the most about, it's no wonder you want 100% certainty that your fears won't come true.

But once essential questions have been asked and answered about your intentions and plans (specifically, the lack thereof) to harm others, and the diagnosis points to OCD, the next step is to take the scary leap of treating it like it's OCD even when some doubt remains.

Common Obsessive Thoughts in the Fear of Impulsive Harm

- What if I respond to an impulse to grab a weapon (or a device that could be a weapon, like a pen) and use it on someone?

- What if I push someone into danger (for example, off a train platform)?

- What if I lunge for someone's throat or eyes?

- What if I am suddenly inspired by something I see to commit a violent act against someone?

- What if someone causes me to become angry and my anger is uncontrollably expressed through violence?

Common Compulsions in the Fear of Impulsive Harm

- Reciting neutralizing thoughts or prayers to protect from hurting anyone

- Avoiding any TV or movies that have even the slightest amount of violence in them

- Hiding or disposing of any knives, scissors, or even pencils that could be used as a weapon

- Refusing to sit within reaching distance of people, in case you were to lunge at them

- Avoiding walking near people on the sidewalk, in case you were to push someone into traffic

- Reassurance seeking that you would never "snap" and harm someone

- Confessing thoughts, urges, or perceived impulses to harm people

- Reading and rereading articles on the Internet about why people snap

- Avoiding being alone with triggering people (anyone deemed a potential victim)

- Avoiding confrontations or people who may generate feelings of anger

- Engaging in safety behaviors to make it more difficult to act violently (for example, locking yourself in a room away from others, wearing thick gloves to impair the ability to grab things, or tying your hands together)

In the guilty-pleasure horror film *Bad Moon*, a man handcuffs himself to a tree during a full moon in the hopes that this will keep his inevitable transformation into a werewolf from harming his family. It doesn't really work (don't worry, the family dog comes to the rescue), but at least his heart's in the right place. People who struggle with this form of Harm OCD often imagine themselves being just on the boundary between being "normal" and a transformation into a beast. The experience is terrifying, like never being able to fully exhale because it might throw you off guard and let the beast out.

But it doesn't have to be this way. Scary as it may be to stand up to this fear of impulsive harm, it is achievable if you implement the right tools. Let's take a look at how the principles of H.E.A.L. can apply.

H: Have Another Look

The hallmark of distorted thinking for the fear of impulsive harm is jumping to unhelpful conclusions. The idea is, if you can't guarantee that *all* of your impulses can be controlled, then you assume that *none* of your impulses can be controlled, meaning that the only moral position is to completely isolate yourself from any person to whom you could cause harm. This is, of course, OCD nonsense. Most people are only mostly in control of most of their impulses most of the time (he writes, with a mouthful of doughnut). The OCD pushes you to make absolutist conclusions based solely on your thoughts and feelings in a given moment. Recognizing how the OCD twists the facts against you can give you the extra space you need to choose not to do compulsions. Here are some examples of what to look out for:

Thought-Action Fusion: *Allowing these thoughts to go unresponded to makes me more likely to act out violently.* That's an easy thing for OCD to say, but where is the evidence? Since you presumably haven't acted out up to this point, entertaining the idea that you will if you don't do compulsions is a choice.

Catastrophizing: *I am going to snap and harm someone, leading to imprisonment or death.* Well, that's a creative idea, but for now that's all we know, that you've had an idea. You can't predict the future. By definition, the problem with acting impulsively is that you can't predict when an urge will overwhelm you into action. Uncomfortable as it may be, we have to stay here in the present. But this also means we have no business assuming that our fear of impulsive harm will come true.

Discounting the Positive: *This time my harm thoughts will come true.* The universe is constantly presenting you with reassuring information in the form of you not having harmed anyone. The OCD wants to discount that information by saying this moment is different. Though we can't prove otherwise, we also shouldn't ignore the reality that contradicts it.

Tunnel Vision: *I noticed that knife because I'm going to use it!* Could be, or maybe, more likely, you noticed the knife because you have an obsession with knives.

Emotional Reasoning: *This tension and anxiety I feel means I am going to push someone into the street.* It's unclear what our feelings are trying to tell us, if indeed they are trying to tell us anything. Tension is tension. Thinking that tension is a predictor of a feared act is adding OCD's narrative to the equation.

Shoulds: *I should always be confident that I can control my impulses.* The trick here is to notice the crafty language of your OCD. Impulses are, by definition, experiences that come up out of your control. Responding to them is within your control, but this has nothing to do with confidence. The OCD chips away at your confidence to con you into doing compulsions.

E: Exposure and Response Prevention

Exposure and response prevention approaches to the fear of impulsive harm may seem impossible. *If I'm afraid of killing my wife in the middle of the night, how can I do exposure to that without, um, y'know...?* The key here is to recognize that the OCD has you trapped in content (the scary words that make up your thoughts) instead of the process of how you relate to those scary words. Exposing yourself to these fears simply means putting yourself in situations where the fears are likely to be present and practicing being there with them without doing compulsions. In Harm OCD, it's always a good idea to do a mix of in vivo exposures (doing things that are triggering) and imaginal exposures (writing scripts that are triggering). In his book *Freedom from Obsessive Compulsive Disorder*, Jonathan Grayson reminds us that "falling within the OCD diagnosis doesn't mean you won't engage in violence. Remember, the goal isn't to be reassured, but to take a risk" (2003, 203). In other words, ERP is about training yourself to respond differently to your unwanted thoughts and to learn to live without certainty, the way people without OCD do. First, let's review the rules again for effective ERP.

Important Rules for ERP

- **Don't do exposure in a manner where accidental harm is likely to take place.** In the case of impulsive harm obsessions, a good example of an unacceptable exposure would be holding a loaded firearm without training and without the supervision of someone who is trained.

- **You don't have to violate your values in the name of ERP.** If you have a fear of shooting someone and part of your value system includes being opposed to gun owner-ship, then buying a gun for exposure purposes is not an acceptable ERP strategy because it requires you to go against your values. Doing ERP with fake guns, stores where guns are sold, media involving guns, and imaginal exposures or scripts about using a gun are just as effective, if not more so.

- **No testing.** The purpose of ERP is *not* to prove that you won't act out and harm someone. The purpose of ERP is to learn to accept uncertainty and to change the way you respond to your unwanted thoughts about harm. Often this means paying attention to what you are telling your-self during an exposure. Standing near someone on a subway platform when you have a fear of pushing people in front of trains is a good exposure. However, if you are simultaneously telling yourself *See? I'm not going to do it*, then you are just doing an extensive checking ritual.

In Vivo Exposure Tips

The key to in vivo ERP for fear of impulsive harm is doing every-thing you can to eliminate the argument that you are incapable of causing harm. In other words, by removing all the barriers to harming people, you insist that the brain accept uncertainty. Some examples include:

- Safely and legally carrying a concealed weapon (for example, a pocket knife)

- Chopping food or using a blender in the kitchen

- Driving while allowing harm thoughts

- Standing near people at the edge of a street or subway platform

- Keeping hands out of pockets when alone with someone

- Visiting a sporting goods store where you could buy a weapon

- Watching movies with triggering scenes of spontaneous acts of violence

- Playing violent video games

All of the above are heightened in their effectiveness if done around triggering people. If your Harm OCD focuses intensely on one particular person, such as a spouse, then agreeing with your unwanted thoughts as exposure when in your spouse's presence can be very effective. Being alone with your spouse, and in particular being alone in triggering environments, can also be helpful. For example, you could go hiking with your wife in an area where a simple push could bring your fears to life.

Acceptance and Motivation Scripts

This style of scripting helps prepare you for the big fight ahead with OCD. Exposure to a fear of impulsively harming people means exposure to the potential of impulsively harming people. We are usually taught to be less impulsive or to take more care in our actions to avoid causing harm. But to overcome this form of OCD, this learning has gone too far and needs to be scaled back. Recognizing that your efforts to be certain you won't harm anyone will always fail to satisfy the OCD means you can start investing in life instead of living in fear. Start by addressing what you are going to do that the OCD won't like, and then describe how this makes it possible that your fears could come true. Then identify what you think is likely to happen if you try the impossible task of getting certainty that all of your impulses are controlled. Lastly, consider what it is you really care about that would make you take this risk of getting better.

An Example of an Acceptance and Motivation Script: "I'm going to start spending more time in public settings. I'm going to stop avoiding situations where I might be alone with people. I'm going to stand near people on the subway platform. This lack of vigilance in compulsive avoidance could leave me vulnerable to an impulse that causes me to harm someone. I may push someone off the subway platform and kill them. I may have to be institutionalized or put away for being a danger to society. But if I continue to obey my OCD, I will become increasingly isolated and continue to convince myself that I am a ticking time bomb. I will cut myself off completely from those I love and will fall into a pit of depression and confusion. I still won't know for sure whether I might snap and hurt someone. I value being a social person who can shake hands and network and bring people together. I am an affectionate and loving person and if it takes having thoughts about hurting people to be able to get close to them, then I choose the thoughts over the avoidance. I choose life over servitude to OCD."

Flooding Scripts

Remember that this style of scripting is designed to get you thirsty for compulsions. It is that thirst that you are trying to master because quenching it with rituals is taking too much of what you care about away from you. A good way to do flooding scripts for a fear of impulsive harm is to describe the consequences of letting the impulses win. The more detail you can use and the more specific you can be about the victim(s) of your violent crime, the more powerful this exercise can be. The example below may be immensely triggering for some readers, so please proceed with caution. That being said, consider that I wrote this with a cat in my lap.

An Example of a Flooding Script: "I can't take it anymore. I decide to start agreeing with the thoughts and realize more and more that doing whatever I feel like in the moment is fine by me. I get the thought about stabbing my wife, so I get up and go down to the kitchen to get the biggest knife we have. I clutch it tightly in my hands and take it up to the bedroom. My wife is sleeping comfortably in the bed. I walk over to her and abruptly plunge the knife into her chest. It is harder to get the knife in than I thought, so I have to push hard on the handle to get past her sternum and cut all the way through to the mattress beneath her. Her eyes shoot wide open and she screams. It takes a few seconds for her to realize that she has been stabbed. She looks at me in horror. She tries to speak, but blood just pours from her mouth. Her eyes tell me she always knew I was going to do it and her last thought is anger at me for deceiving her this long. Blood vessels in her eyes begin to burst and then I see her pupils turn gray. I step away, blood all over my hands, and begin to realize what I have done. I feel horrible. I want to take it back, but I can't. I pick up the phone to call the police and confess. I struggle to hold the phone because my hands are slippery with my dead wife's blood. I dial 911 and say, 'I killed my wife. It was me. I did it.' The police come and arrest me. I am given life in prison and spend the rest of my days alone in a cell thinking about what I could have done to avoid snapping. I never get a satisfying answer and my entire existence is made up of the repeated image of my knife plunging into her flesh."

Okay, that was intense, I know. Take a few deep breaths and acknowledge that you just did something courageous. Letting yourself be in the presence of such terrifying and grotesque thoughts is going to generate some notable discomfort. Remember that using a technique like this in your fight against OCD means choosing to get in the ring with discomfort and learning to make space for it without compulsions.

A: Acceptance and Mindfulness

Mindfulness for the fear of impulsive harm means learning to observe the rising and falling of impulses and thoughts about impulses as they occur organically. We may not like it, but as human beings, we naturally have violent impulses that rise within us. Typically, we trust that a mechanism in our brain can quickly assess when to actively suppress an impulse and when to essentially ignore it. OCD interferes with that trust and tries to task you with the ultimate responsibility of perfectly assessing and judging everything that looks like a violent impulse. So the first thing to remember about being mindful of this kind of Harm OCD is to be mindful of the brain's natural process of allowing impulses to rise and fall without being acted on. This requires staying present with those impulses (or with what look like impulses to you) and resisting the urge to neutralize them prematurely with compulsions. Instead, let them come and go without compulsions and view them simply as objects of attention passing by. When you do this, you are likely to become aware of commentary in the mind, things like, *If you let yourself feel this any longer, you're going to snap*, or, *You are being reckless and irresponsible by allowing this impulse to go unchecked.* Simply note that these are thoughts and let them come and go. They are like the little fish that clean the sharks as they swim by in the aquarium. Notice them and let them keep swimming.

It's very common for people with this manifestation of Harm OCD to worry a lot about the distinction between an unwanted thought and an urge. The OCD may try to bully you into seeking certainty by demanding that you review your experience over and over again, collect reassurance from others (or the Internet), and be perfectly satisfied that your thoughts are not urges or desires. Try to remember that this futile quest for certainty is just more thinking about your thoughts and feelings. It doesn't lead to freedom from your obsession. The problem here isn't a lack of information. It's not the content of your thoughts, but the activity of thinking that is getting you stuck. Mindfulness asks that you simply note the "thinking" and allow it to be as it is.

Another aspect of mindfulness for the fear of impulsive harm is observing that you have a marvelously creative mind. So in addition to being mindful of the natural rising and falling of violent or pseudoviolent impulses, you want to also view these entire *stories*, these new and exciting ways of hurting people that your OCD comes up with, as objects of attention. Though they do not reflect your identity or your morals and they are not predictors of your behavior, these thoughts are nonetheless *your* thoughts happening in *your* mind. Viewing them as the mind simply wandering into peculiar territory, as it often does, will keep you in command of your OCD and less likely to respond with compulsions.

In meditation, you may quickly notice that resting your attention anywhere seems to bring out a whole lot of demons in the mind. Don't be too distracted by the gory or horrific nature of the images that pop up in these quiet moments. View them as challenges to acceptance and let them be ideas that you are willing to make space for. You may be resting your attention on the breath and then your mind naturally wanders off (as it is inclined to do) and then you find yourself attending to an image of a loved one being violently harmed. You may instinctively want to analyze it and make sure you are disgusted by it enough, or maybe you want to flee from it and block it out with some happy thought. This state is called being distracted. All you need to know about the violent thought is that it is not your breath. Then return to the breath. Remember, meditation is the development of this skill—knowing when you are distracted by your thoughts and feelings, and returning to the present moment without conditions or compulsions.

L: Love and Self-Compassion

It's essential to remember that OCD uses self-criticism as a tool. It's not some incidental thing, as if people with OCD are too hard on themselves for no reason. Rather, OCD thrives on compulsions, and compulsions are strategies for reducing the discomfort you have with your unwanted thoughts. By pushing your buttons, OCD manipulates you into thinking you need to self-soothe with compulsions. One way it does this is by repeatedly shining a light on your least self-loving ideas. *You're disgusting for thinking this. You're a monster for even wondering about this.* And so the OCD wears you down and makes compulsions seem inevitable. Again, by countering this with self-compassion, you can take the power back from your OCD.

Remember, like it or not, your mind takes you to some wild places. So why not like it—or at least respect it? Instead of hating yourself for thinking and feeling like you could harm someone, why not embrace this creativity? Viewing your OCD as something trying to entertain you, instead of something trying to destroy you, can be an act of self-love.

Using the tenets of self-compassion described in chapter 2, you can construct coping statements to help you resist compulsions: mindfulness (acknowledging that you are having the thoughts and feelings that you are having); common humanity (reminding yourself that other people have similar experiences); and self-kindness (reminding yourself that there are plenty of things you are doing right and that you can cut yourself some slack without doing compulsions).

An Example of a Coping Statement: "I'm having intrusive thoughts about hurting people at this family picnic and I'm feeling afraid and guilty. Many people with OCD struggle with these kinds of thoughts, and even people without OCD would find this kind of mental imagery upsetting. I'm doing a decent job recognizing that this is OCD and trying my best not to give in to compulsions. I need to give myself permission to have these kinds of thoughts and choose to let them come and go as best I can while I invite myself to engage with others at this picnic."

You're Not Crazy

It's easy to underestimate the amount of strength it takes to live with the fear of impulsive harm in OCD. Each day can feel like a game of Russian roulette wherein you are constantly asked to pull the trigger on your life, and though all you ever get is a click, it always feels like the next one will be the bullet. The truth is, with the right treatment, you can regain confidence in your ability to assess how seriously you should take unwanted violent thoughts. You may come to realize that thinking the way you do is more like having a great horror novelist in your head than it is like being some kind of loose cannon. Who knows, you may even learn to appreciate the novelist in your head instead of devoting precious time and attention to condemning it.

Recap

H: Have Another Look. Distorted thinking leads you to the false belief that the presence of any individual thought or feeling is a sure sign that you are going to hurt, or are capable of hurting, someone, and that you need to avoid or neutralize such thoughts in order to keep a violent act from occurring. Recognizing these thought traps for what they are can help you to resist compulsions.

E: Exposure and Response Prevention. It's scary stuff, but it works. Done well, in vivo exposure to situations where impulsive acts of harm could do some real damage can be very effective. Gradually working your way up a hierarchy of feared situations while resisting safety behaviors can put you back in command of your OCD. Watching or reading stories about snapping and writing scripts about losing control and hurting others and having to cope with the consequences can free you from your fear and teach you that you really are capable of accepting uncertainty about your violent thoughts.

A: Acceptance and Mindfulness. The better you are at observing what's on the screen of your mind, the easier it is to see obsessive thoughts, feelings, and impulses about harming people as background actors in an otherwise watchable movie of your life. Remember that thinking about the difference between unwanted thoughts and "urges" is still just more thinking. Getting into the meditation process when you have Harm OCD can be scary. Don't be discouraged when your early experiences with it include closing your eyes and seeing a lot of carnage.

L: Love and Self-Compassion. You have so much compassion for others, you even worry about harm that hasn't happened to them! Syphon off some of that compassion and turn it inward. If the OCD can't tear you down with name-calling and shaming, then it leaves you in a position to fight this thing and win it.

CHAPTER 5

Fear of Self-Harm

Many people with Harm OCD suffer intensely trying to cope with the uncertainty about whether they would or could harm another person. One compulsive strategy for relieving this anxiety might be to avoid the target of your unwanted thoughts, avoid the people you fear harming. But what if it were truly impossible to avoid that person? What if the imagined victim is you?

You've probably been asked before, "What's the worse that can happen?" and your response left the asker sorry to have asked! Living with OCD often means being frustratingly aware of the worst that could happen in a given situation. This naturally lends itself to intrusive images of reckless disregard, such as jumping off of things, spontaneously cutting or hitting yourself, grabbing a handful of pills, and so on. Anyone with OCD is likely to come up with these kinds of fringe ideas when prompted (or when not prompted). It's one of the things you're really exceptional at: noticing the fringe! But when the content relates directly to your specific obsession, it's hard to view this thinking style as a skill set.

Intrusive self-harm thoughts in OCD may be more pronounced when one is faced with stress, unwanted obligations, shame, and so on. So in some cases they may present themselves as frustrating magnifications of negative thoughts about yourself (similar to other violent thoughts that naturally arise toward others in frustrated states, as discussed earlier). But in most cases of self-harm OCD, these thoughts intrude independently from any depressive symptoms or other cues that would make one wonder about suicidal thoughts. In other words, they are totally ego dystonic intruders (that is, they don't line up with your identity as you understand it), and part of what makes them so upsetting is the random nature of the intrusions.

Fear of violent self-harm often connects with a fear of emotional harm to others, so it isn't far removed from the fear of harboring a harmful identity discussed in chapter 3. You may obsess about hurting yourself in part because you know how devastating it would be to those who care about you. Having this power to ruin not only your own life, but the lives of everyone around you, can be overwhelming. *What if I did it? What if I just turned my car into oncoming traffic? What if I just cut my throat right here in this moment, without provocation, for no reason at all? What if I just eliminated myself, leaving my loved ones alone to fend for themselves in perpetual misery?* Strategies to prove that you won't harm yourself can lead to extreme avoidance and failure to function. If *anything* can be used to harm yourself, even your own hands, how can you ever feel truly safe? Safety in this context is not the absence of danger. Safety is the emotional state you find when you are able to rest your attention in uncertainty and live meaningfully without proof of the absence of harm. But when OCD demands certainty that you are safe from harming yourself, it can make an argument that *any* state of being alive represents a danger. You get stuck in a loop. Prove that you will stay alive, but eliminate all aspects of life that could be threatening? Impossible!

Near the beginning of this book I gave the example of Elizabeth, who got stuck on the thought that she could jump out of a window and then later obsessed about harming herself through poison and other means. Step by step she stripped away all of the things from her life that scared her, but this meant stripping away all of the things that made her really value life in the first place. She then gets trapped in the OCD argument that life may not be worth living, which then becomes a trigger for fearing that she could harm herself. If you, like Elizabeth, struggle with self-harm thoughts, you may have spent a long time feeling like you're never free to fully relax, because your mind tells you that at any moment, you could snap and kill yourself. It can be pretty isolating. If you try to talk about it, people may assume that you're suicidal (and you're not always sure that you're not). Let's look at some basic concepts for assessing any reasons for concern beyond OCD.

Assessing for Safety

There is a natural tendency in OCD treatment circles to view the content of thoughts as meaningless. There's good reason for this. Thoughts are only thoughts; it is our reaction to them that causes problems. That being said, we therapists perk our ears right up when we hear the words, "I'm having thoughts of harming myself." It's just something we have to deal with as humans because most of us live in a society where we naturally care if another person lives or dies. But therapists go through a lot of training that focuses on determining whether or not a client is safe and whether or not we might need to intervene to keep the client safe. It may come as no surprise that being an OCD therapist with OCD makes this aspect of my profession somewhat daunting. When I hear "I am having thoughts about hurting myself," I want to know almost as much as my client does whether or not we're *really* talking about OCD. No individual facet of the following questions necessarily means cause for alarm, but exploring each of these with a mental health professional is an important first step. The idea is to build a three-dimensional picture of your mental and emotional status wherein the therapist, as an outside observer, can make an educated assumption about your safety.

- Do you have a committed desire to harm yourself, and if so, what is your specific reason behind it?

- Do you have a specific plan for harming yourself?

- Is there a specific point in time you imagine doing this?

- Do you have a history of attempting self-harm or suicide, and if so, what were the specifics of those attempts?

- Have you been recently exposed to a traumatic event?

- Are you severely depressed or bipolar?

- Do you take medication, are you taking it as prescribed, and have these thoughts coincided with any recent changes in your medication?

If you answered "yes" to any of the first three questions, better to go to your nearest emergency room, and then deal with any OCD that may also be involved after you are safe.

The Suicide Compulsion?

Most of the OCD sufferers I have met, with or without Harm OCD, describe having at least some thoughts about suicide. Though suicide is an important risk factor specifically for people with harm OCD (Ching, Williams, and Siev 2017), sometimes the suicide thought is not so much intrusive as it is just a place the OCD sufferer directs his attention to as a strategy to avoid thinking about an obsession. With all of these bright lights shining on terrible thoughts, one can't help but wonder what it might be like if all the lights were turned off. If you imagine a world where you don't have any unwanted thoughts, then naturally there is only one world that fits that description: death. So you might have found yourself *compulsively* thinking about suicide in order to avoid thinking about another obsession. This may also be looked at as a form of self-reassurance from imagined future guilt, as in "If these thoughts come true, I'll just kill myself."

It cannot be stressed enough that proper assessment of the manner and intention behind suicidal thinking should take place at the beginning of treatment, as well as at various points throughout treatment. A professional mental health provider should carefully examine the way you respond to your thoughts and help you sort out what you believe about the thoughts and their power to lead you to self-harm (Golden et al. 2016).

People sometimes withhold discussion of intrusive self-harm thoughts out of fear of being hospitalized against their will. This is an understandable concern, but the best way to address it is to establish trust between you and the therapist through honesty and open dialogue. The more directly you articulate the content of these thoughts and how you relate to them to your therapist, the better the therapist will be able to assess your safety.

Common Obsessive Thoughts in Self-Harm OCD

- I may snap and impulsively
  - cut myself with a knife
  - hang myself
  - turn my car into oncoming traffic
  - jump off a ledge or out of a moving car
  - shoot myself
  - poison myself
  - overdose on my medication
- I may become suicidal by
  - being alone for too long
  - letting myself experience sadness or stress
  - letting myself be exposed to things that are upsetting
  - letting myself feel less than perfectly in control

Common Compulsions in Self-Harm OCD

- Avoiding physical triggers
  - Weapons or potentially dangerous objects, chemicals, or pills
  - Ledges that could be jumped from
  - Driving
- Avoiding triggering emotional states (for example, anger, sadness, lack of control)

- Thought neutralization (replacing self-harm thoughts with other thoughts)

- Mental rituals designed to make you feel certain that you won't harm yourself (for example, repeating a list of reasons you want to live, counting, excessive praying)

- Mental analysis of why you would never harm yourself

- Checking to make sure you feel safe or in control

- Checking to make sure you have not done something to harm yourself or have done enough to protect from harming yourself

- Seeking reassurance from others, the Internet, or self-reassurance, including confessing thoughts to elicit commentary that you are safe

- Avoiding all references to suicide in media (for example, music by artists who have committed suicide, movies with scenes related to suicide)

The OCD wants you to devote your life to making sure you don't lose your life, by accident, out of impulse, or with intention. But efforts to be certain you will not harm yourself always end up fueling greater doubt in the end and only result in doing more compulsions. If you are desperately trying to prove that you won't harm yourself, your brain can only conclude that you are unsure about your safety and that intrusive thoughts about self-harm are automatically important. Let's take a look at HEALing ways to stand up to this kind of Harm OCD.

H: Have Another Look

Like the fear of impulsive harm toward others discussed in the previous chapter, fear of impulsively harming yourself can be intensified by faulty thinking about the significance of your triggers. Remember, the

OCD "wants" you to think of compulsions as necessary, not as optional. Recognizing how the OCD is confusing you on this issue is one way to overcome it.

Thought-Action Fusion: *If I allow this thought to go unchecked, it will make me more likely to commit suicide.* Remember that thoughts are not physical objects that stack up and create mass. There is no limit to the frequency or number of times you have a thought where it automatically stops being just a thought and definitely starts being a predictor of behavior.

Catastrophizing: *If I go to the roof, I will jump to my death.* It's ironic that the OCD says in one breath that you need to be extravigilant because you can't predict if you might snap and lose your life and then in the next breath tells you to avoid engaging with life because of the prediction that you will snap and cause harm. Lose-lose. Remind yourself that the future is unknown, and ask yourself if there is something on the roof that you want.

Discounting the Positive: *This one thought about self-harm feels real and all the other ones before it were just OCD.* It's always "this time," so don't let your history of being able to keep yourself safe get tossed away over a momentary thought or feeling.

Tunnel Vision: *Robin Williams committed suicide so anybody can at any moment, including me.* Other people who are not you, going through life experiences that you are not going through and making choices that you have not made, are not a reason to condemn yourself to being a slave to OCD. Notice that you *notice* these stories above all others because that's what your OCD does.

Emotional Reasoning: *I feel nervous, therefore I cannot be trusted around this knife not to cut myself.* Remember that you often feel nervous or guilty for literally no reason other than that this is what it feels like to have OCD. How you feel is not a reliable indicator of what behaviors you will choose.

Shoulds: *I should never have a thought about harming myself.* Remember here that the problem with the "should" is that it takes basically healthy ideas and makes them so rigid that you cannot tolerate them. There are certainly better ways to spend your attention than on your unwanted suicide-themed mental junkmail. But given that self-harm exists in the known universe, it makes sense that you may think of it from time to time. Barring yourself from having any kind of thought is the best way to invite more OCD into your life.

E: Exposure and Response Prevention

Exposures to your unwanted self-harm thoughts and to things that could potentially be used to cause yourself harm can be very effective, especially if they are things you are likely to encounter in your life anyway, such as knives. Reducing unnecessary or excessively compulsive safety behaviors can also play an important role. As discussed in the previous chapter, there are three essentially important rules that must be respected in doing this kind of ERP.

Important Rules for ERP

- **Don't do exposure in a manner where accidental harm is likely.** An example of unnecessary risk here might be stepping over a guardrail at the edge of a cliff and standing there with your arms outstretched and your eyes closed. It hopefully goes without saying that hurting yourself is not how you overcome a fear of hurting yourself, and neither is putting yourself in situations where you are likely to be hurt. Fear is overcome by learning to live with uncertainty.

- **You don't have to violate your values in the name of ERP.** For example, if you have a fear of harming yourself by losing control while under the influence of alcohol and your value system doesn't include drinking, then it is better to use imaginal forms of ERP.

- **No testing.** The purpose of exposure is not to prove to yourself that you won't hurt yourself. It is to prove that you are capable of sitting with uncertainty and investing your attention in more than just your OCD. Though it may seem logical to push a knife against your skin to see if you would "really" do it, this behavior is actually compulsive certainty-seeking, and compulsions make OCD worse. Testing compulsions can also lead to accidental harm and values-opposing behaviors, violating the rules mentioned above.

In Vivo Exposure Tips

Everything that follows assumes that you have been properly assessed for suicidality and are not at meaningful risk of self-harm according to a professional evaluation. I use the word "meaningful" here only to emphasize that uncertainty is pervasive and we all have to make space for the possibility of being wrong.

REMOVING SAFETY BEHAVIORS

If you have hidden the knives or pills or other instruments you imagine harming yourself with, get them out in the open. Remember, teaching your brain that you can be in the presence of these thoughts without doing compulsions is how you get better. It follows then that doing things that bring these thoughts to the forefront and then resisting compulsive response to them is an effective OCD-fighting strategy. You may want to start by simply putting things you've hidden back where they belong (for example, putting pills back in the medicine cabinet). Taking the ERP challenge a step further, you might put them on your nightstand or kitchen counter in plain view (assuming this is otherwise safe and not risking children accessing anything dangerous).

Similarly, you might practice keeping a pocket knife with you, parking on the top floor of a parking structure, or leaving belts or ropes lying about, depending on what kind of thoughts your OCD likes to bully you with.

BRING ON THE THOUGHTS

Your OCD is a dictator and, like all dictators, it is insecure. It wants to control what you watch, what you listen to, and what you talk about so you don't get any "ideas" about freedom from oppression. Watching movies where characters commit suicide, listening to music by artists who have committed suicide, and reading books and articles about suicide (without seeking reassurance) are all good exposure strategies. If holding something like a knife also brings on the thoughts, then do so, but remember that any sort of exposure in this style should not be used to test what will happen. You need to be able to sit with the thoughts of "I might do it." Exposures like these should be first practiced with the guidance of a professional.

LEARN TO BE ALONE

You may fear that if you are alone, your harm thoughts will overwhelm you and you may use the presence of others as a form of reassurance that you are being monitored and can't hurt yourself. Gradually increasing your exposure to being alone can be really scary. However, it can also be really effective and a way to reacquaint yourself with what makes you, well, you. Binge-watch Netflix, cook yourself chilaquiles, wear slippers, sing and dance to your favorite songs. In other words, practice being free and being "okay alone" even with your unwanted thoughts. ERP does not necessitate being miserable.

Acceptance and Motivation Scripts

If you have this self-harm form of OCD, you have to deal with two competing and yet equally nasty voices in your head. One tells you that you're going to harm yourself even though you don't want to. The other one tells you that living this way is unbearable and the only way out is probably suicide. These are not two voices truly, but two *tones* of voice that the OCD uses to keep you enslaved. Overcoming self-harm OCD means choosing to release yourself from the contract to find certainty and instead investing in the real life you actually do have. For this script, start by acknowledging that you're giving up the quest for certainty and some (or all) of the behaviors that go with that. Then describe what you might be risking in making this choice. Be brief, but be direct about the fact that you may harm yourself (remember, this is part of the exposure). Then describe what you think your life will look like if you devote it entirely to proving that you won't harm yourself. What kind of life will that be? Lastly, reflect on what makes this fight so worth it.

An Example of an Acceptance and Motivation Script: "I am going to stop trying to prove to myself that I won't commit suicide. I am going to stop avoiding knives and will start doing exposure to them and using them in the kitchen. I am going to start listening to Nirvana again and accept that this may come with thoughts of hurting myself. This may result in me losing the plot and deciding in a split second to harm myself. This could happen by me slitting my wrists, and my family may find me in a pool of blood in the bathtub. Because if I continue to obey my OCD and keep trying to get certainty about my harming thoughts, I will continue to isolate myself from society. I will keep avoiding knives and music and other things that bring about the thoughts, but this will just make the thoughts more intrusive. I will spend every waking moment in my head trying to prove that I won't hurt myself and I will still fail. Eventually, unable to function, I will probably become massively depressed and may even become truly suicidal. I was taught to love life and to cherish the moments we have on this earth. I value being a loving wife and mother. I want to be present for my child as he grows up and not always in my head. It's worth it for me to take the risk of stopping compulsions and accepting uncertainty because OCD simply does not offer me the life I can have."

Flooding Scripts

As with the fear of impulsively harming others, a good way to get into the ring with your self-harm OCD is to describe your fear coming true in detail and try to sit with the experience without doing any mental rituals to self-reassure. The more brutal and direct you can be, the more impactful the script may be. Just remember that the aim is to get yourself into a fearful state where you become aware of the urge to do compulsions and you resist that urge. Don't fall for the trap of rationalizing throughout your script and using it to prove that your fears won't come true. As always, use it to prove that you are capable of being in the presence of fear without compulsions. The following may be considerably triggering, so proceed with caution.

An Example of a Flooding Script: "I drive to the top of the parking structure and get out of the car. I go to the edge by the railing and look out on a view of the entire city. I climb over the railing and let my toes dangle over the edge. I look down several hundred feet to the sidewalk. I close my eyes and start to lean forward. Eventually, gravity takes over and my body tips and falls over the edge and begins to plummet toward the earth. I can feel the air in my face as I careen toward the ground. I feel confused, like I've made a terrible mistake but like I've been finally freed from my burdens at the same time. The ground draws nearer and then my body crashes into the unyielding concrete. The bones in my skull, back, arms, and legs are all crushed. A pool of blood forms around my body. I am not dead yet. I feel incredible pain from every nerve as the darkness slowly swallows me. I made a mistake. I want to take it back. It hurts so much. People are screaming. Some people come over to see and gasp at the horror. I can't see, but I can hear. Then I can't hear. Then I can't feel. Then I am gone. After I pass, my family is informed and they are devastated."

A: Acceptance and Mindfulness

Being mindful of unwanted self-harm thoughts means giving yourself enough distance from problem solving and *thinking* to be able to observe the thoughts forming, demanding attention, and then passing. If you incorporate meditation and other forms of mindfulness training into your treatment, you may improve your ability to be a nonjudgmental observer of these thoughts and be able to return your attention to the things you care about in the present moment, and not just to your obsessions. If you are new to meditation, don't be surprised by a sudden heightening of your unwanted thoughts when you sit and practice. The first step to meditating is often asking yourself to rest the attention on the breath. For people with OCD, this often gets interpreted as "Don't think harm thoughts," which makes such thoughts more likely to intrude. The key to meditating effectively and developing your mindfulness skills is simply to be aware of the rising and falling of your self-harm thoughts and to consistently begin again by returning your attention to the breath, again and again.

But don't leave this just for meditating. Remember, meditation is the practice of an exercise, but learning to map this onto your daily life is the key. In other words, by positioning yourself as an observer, not a victim, of your thoughts, you can engage in the things you value, recognize the self-harm intrusions as simply thoughts, and return from their distraction without having to engage in rituals.

L: Love and Self-Compassion

Self-harm OCD can come at you from multiple angles at the same time. It says that you will hurt yourself when you don't want to. But thinking about hurting yourself all day is likely to make you unhappy. It doesn't have to if you can view thoughts as meaningless objects of attention, but we're not born naturally adept at this. We're born to seek out threats to ourselves and eliminate them, perhaps even if the so-called threats are just our thoughts. Never forget how brave you are for living with OCD and trying to cope with someone in your head that keeps threatening to kill you.

This means that to be self-compassionate about self-harm obsessions, you have to start by understanding that this *really just is hard*. You may think of yourself as weak or foolish for worrying about your intrusive harm thoughts. Or maybe you think you're crazy or going to lose it. The truth is the opposite. You're not crazy. By recognizing how much of you there is to love, you simultaneously create an environment where your OCD is just OCD, your thoughts are just thoughts, and your ability to overcome your challenges is without limits. Interacting compassionately with your mind means talking to yourself as you would to a good friend. Teasing is allowed as long as it isn't mean-spirited. If you can use humor to relate to the darkest of thoughts, you can help yourself through the darkest of times.

As always, when constructing self-compassion coping statements, try to think about the most honest description of what's happening. It isn't necessarily the happiest, but it also should be void of criticism. Acknowledge that you are having the thoughts and feelings that you're having. Recognize that others do (or at least would) find these thoughts and feelings difficult to contend with. Then invite yourself to recognize your strengths and your ability to exert those strengths against the OCD.

An Example of a Coping Statement: "I'm having a lot of intrusive thoughts today and I'm afraid I'll snap and hurt myself. Many people would find thoughts of self-harm disturbing and be frustrated by them intruding. I'm doing a decent job of resisting overt compulsions right now. I need to give myself permission to view this as something I'm still working on and invite myself to write an exposure script and then reward myself for the hard work with a good jog."

You're Not Crazy

People get self-harming thoughts. Sometimes they manifest as a response to internal desperation. Sometimes they manifest as a fantasy of not having to think horrible thoughts. Sometimes they intrude for literally no reason other than that you have OCD. Obsessing about self-harm is no weirder or less treatable than obsessing about germs or anything else. Remember that the OCD wants to isolate you from others and tells you that you're different, so that you continue to work for it like a slave. Learning to stand up against this bully and fight for your peace of mind takes great strength. If you're reading this, then you have this strength.

Recap

H: Have Another Look. Having unwanted thoughts of self-harm does not automatically mean you are in danger. OCD uses trickery to push you into assuming the worst. Stepping back and noticing that you are being tricked by the way in which you look at these thoughts can give you the advantage you need to choose not to do compulsions.

E: Exposure and Response Prevention. Self-harm exposures are scary, but then so are all exposures. In vivo exposure to being around things you imagine you could harm yourself with, and eliminating safety behaviors, can put the OCD in its place. Writing scripts about harming yourself can also be very effective, but be on the lookout for mental rituals or rationalizations that might render them less impactful.

A: Acceptance and Mindfulness. Admitting to yourself that these are the thoughts that are going through your head can often feel like a major exposure. But learning to be a better nonjudgmental observer of your self-harm thoughts can help you see them as objects of your attention, not threats to your safety.

L: Love and Self-Compassion. OCD does its best to make you hate yourself and then tells you that you are more likely to commit an act of self-harm because of these hateful feelings. Approaching yourself with love, compassion, and a sense of humor (even dark humor), can help you turn the tables on your OCD.

CHAPTER 6

Fear of Harming Children

It's commonly understood that OCD goes after the things we love the most. When we worry and obsess about harm coming to people in our lives, we worry first about those closest to us. Then we divide people into degrees of perceived vulnerability. We worry hardest about those whom we are charged with protecting and keeping safe. OCD going after your children can be tragically debilitating. How can parents connect to the joy of parenting if they cannot feel at peace in the presence of their child?

It's totally unfair. It takes so many effortful commitments to get to the place in life where you can call yourself a mom or a dad, and then right at the moment when you start to truly appreciate how amazing that is, OCD swoops in for the kill (as it were). It may not come as a surprise. If you've been living with OCD for some time, you've likely seen it go after your relationships, your sexual orientation, your health anxieties, your sense of safety regarding germs, chemicals, or people in general.

Harm thoughts in mothers can start even before a child is born, manifesting as obsessive concerns about harming the pregnancy or intrusive thoughts of self-harm. Postpartum OCD (where symptoms appear within a month of giving birth) is also common, and if you don't already have a history of OCD, it can appear to come out of nowhere. Changes that take place in the female body during and immediately after pregnancy have a wide range of potential effects on one's mental health and emotional stability. It is unclear why some people see a notable increase in their OCD symptoms during and after pregnancy and some people don't (or even see the opposite). What we do know is that when postpartum OCD occurs, it most often manifests as unwanted intrusive thoughts of aggression against the child (Abramowitz et al. 2003b).

Whether you are a mother or father, the OCD can steal your attention with "Will I really do it?" thoughts. It may seem impossible to accept uncertainty that you could harm your child, through negligence or some kind of crack in your morality. But recall from the discussion in chapter 2 that uncertainty reigns supreme, even in things we care the most about. You may be so consumed by your fears of harming your children that you overlook the actually harm caused by obeying the OCD. For example:

- Lack of physical affection due to fear of contact

- Lack of physical presence due to avoidance

- Lack of mental presence due to being "in your head" all the time

- Conflict between you and your coparent due to anxiety and the imbalance in parental involvement

- Lack of healthy bond between parent and child due to association of child with mental anguish

The list above is not meant to make you feel guilty, but angry. Near the beginning of this book, I used the example of Richard, who was plagued with intrusive images of shooting his infant son. You may find yourself wishing for some other kind of OCD. There is a sense of "No, not this, anything but this." Perhaps it is because you know that you will probably always have your child in your life, so you imagine being unhappy indefinitely unless you get certainty about the thought. Or maybe you think that your thoughts about children are representative of the worst kind of person one could be, and the guilt and shame this induces makes it uniquely overwhelming.

Assessing for Safety

Revealing that you have intrusive thoughts about harming a child can be terrifying. Treatment professionals in the US are mandated reporters by the state in which they are licensed. This means that they are required by law to contact a child services agency when there is a reasonable suspicion that a child is in danger. The word "reasonable" is left up to the professional to determine. You may fear that your child is in danger just because of your thoughts, but in fact the opposite is true when you have Harm OCD. Your fear of causing harm to your child makes you overprotective or avoidant, which is a completely different problem. Questions that need to be explored carefully with a treatment professional include:

- Do you use physical discipline in your household, and if so, specifically how?

- Have you ever physically harmed a child intentionally?

- Do you have a history of committing acts of violent aggression?

- Do your unwanted thoughts present themselves as thoughts, commands, or voices?

Again, no individual answer to the above questions is an automatic deal breaker, but a careful examination of the answers may be important. Given the delicate nature of these types of discussions, it is extremely important to make sure you are being assessed by a treatment provider who specializes in OCD and knows what to look for.

Common Obsessive Thoughts in the Fear of Harming Children:

- What if I kill or physically harm my child by stabbing, shaking, strangling, smothering, drowning, disposing of him in the trash, or placing her in a harmful situation?

- What if I "snap" and go crazy, or respond to an unwanted impulse that leads to attacking my child?

- What if I harm my child by being willfully or accidentally negligent in a safety measure?

- What if I may have harmed my child and don't know it or blocked it out somehow?

- What if I will never be comfortable with, or will always resent, my child, and associate him or her with these harming thoughts?

- What if I harm my child by being inappropriate with him or her, sexually or otherwise? (Note: This book is primarily focused on the fear of violent harm, but sexual obsessions are also common in OCD and may share territory with harming thoughts.)

Common Compulsions in the Fear of Harming Children:

- Avoidance of:
  - being alone with children
  - bathing, dressing, changing, and so on
  - triggering imagery associated with children
  - schools, parks, and other places children may be present
  - household items that could be used harmfully (knives and so on)
  - objects that are imagined to be harmful or that could be harmful if left unattended or misused (for example, small items that could fall to the ground and be

accidentally ingested, bug spray or cleaning chemicals that could be inadvertently spread to surfaces)

- triggering media (news articles about child harm, movies with related themes, and so on)

- Mental review and other mental rituals to address:

  - Did I touch my child in an inappropriate way?

  - Did I feel an urge to hit or otherwise act aggressively toward my child?

- Reassurance seeking and confessing:

  - Reporting to significant other that you "may have touched" somewhere or done something inappropriate

  - Reporting to significant other that "bad thoughts" occurred

  - Asking others if triggering behaviors, thoughts, or events are "okay" or normal

  - Researching stories of people who have caused harm to children to ensure there are no similarities with yourself

  - Excessive researching of laws and regulations about child safety

  - Self-reassurance (for example, "I would never harm my child because…")

  - Repeated checking to make sure no harm has been done

OCD loves new material and children are, well, new material. One of the deceitful ways the disorder can get you on the hook is by emphasizing the vulnerability of children or the vigilance you need to keep them safe. Fears of harming children are no different from fears of harming anyone else, but even admitting *this* feels like a risky stance to the Harm OCD sufferer with kids. When my first child was born, I thought it quite hilarious that within seconds of her arrival, she was placed before me on a tray and a doctor put a sharp pair of scissors in my hand. It was to cut the umbilical cord. I had an advantage over potential Harm OCD with my children, which is that I always knew full well that I would have intrusive violent thoughts about them. Because I always assumed I'd have thoughts of cutting, smothering, strangling, microwaving them, and so on, I never responded to any individual thought of that nature like it was particularly interesting. If anything, I welcomed such thoughts as useful reminders of why I became a therapist. Let's take a look at how you can apply the principles of HEAL to this form of Harm OCD.

H: Have Another Look

No, you're not going to think your way out of your Harm OCD, but if you can recognize the way you are thinking about your experience and challenge yourself to approach that experience more rationally, it may help you resist compulsions and allow for needed uncertainty. The OCD takes so much, and now it wants your children. Here are some ways it tries to manipulate your thinking to get you to give in:

Thought-Action Fusion: *Allowing violent thoughts about my children means I am a bad person, and that makes them more likely to be harmed.* This idea captures both the morality and probability thinking errors. Thoughts are not actions and confusing the stream of nonsensical data in your mind with moral failing is a distortion cause by your OCD.

Catastrophizing: *If I am left alone with the child, I will harm her.* It is understandably scary to admit that you can't predict the future, but it remains a fact. Don't let your OCD get away with making you think that avoidance of the future is some kind of moral mandate. Remember, "I can't predict the future, but…" can be answered in many ways.

Discounting the Positive: *I could snap at any moment and harm my child, and this moment could be the one.* Sure, it could, but this is an ineffective way to pay attention. People who don't act on their unwanted thoughts tend to continue not acting on their unwanted thoughts.

Tunnel Vision: *I was tense when I strapped my crying child into his car seat and this means I could have abused him.* Any parent without OCD will tell you that you can't sweat the small stuff. There are just too many variables to contend with regarding children and you can't let every single thing be a catastrophe in your mind. OCD wants you to be overly concerned with everything even remotely related to harm fears because it is always building its case against you.

Emotional Reasoning: *I feel disconnected around my child and this means I may not love him enough to keep from harming him.* Since it is impossible to know for sure why you feel anything in any moment, and it is even more elusive to try to make sense of feelings you are checking for, it's better not to use feelings as evidence of potential harm.

Shoulds: *I should only have peaceful and loving thoughts toward my children.* Like all "should" statements, this sounds like a nice idea. But actually, you "should" have a wide variety of thoughts about your children, especially when putting them to bed!

E: Exposure and Response Prevention

The fight for freedom is staged on the battlefield of ERP. The tendency for people who suffer from this form of OCD is to fear ERP as much as they fear their thoughts and feelings. It may seem to you like you are experimenting on your children, putting them at unnecessary risk—even by allowing yourself to "go there" and think those thoughts. But remember the rules of ERP and you'll see things more clearly.

Important Rules for ERP:

- **Don't do exposure in a manner where accidental harm is likely to take place.** If you have a fear of harming your child through negligence, an exposure may be to limit the number of times you check to ensure that her car seat is properly buckled. Maybe you even allow yourself to be distracted by singing a song while you do it. But you don't intentionally leave it unbuckled.

- **You don't have to violate your values in the name of ERP.** As discussed above, you don't actually put children in harm's way to do exposure, but this can be tricky when your harm fears are more abstract. Maybe you are afraid you'll harm your child by exposing him to inappropriate material. The solution to this might be exposure to things slightly out of your comfort zone, but not if they actually go against your values as a parent.

- **No testing.** In the case of obsessions about harming children, a good example of an unacceptable exposure would be briefly holding a pillow over a child's face while she sleeps to prove that you would never push down hard enough to harm her. Even if this causes no actual harm, all it really accomplishes is an added layer of shame about the depths you went to for extreme checking compulsions (not to mention the horror you would both feel if the child woke up in the midst of this). As always, it's essential to remember that the endgame is changing your relationship to uncertainty.

In Vivo Exposure Tips:

- Watching films or reading stories that involve the subject of harming children

- Volunteering for diaper duty and bath time and allowing the harm thoughts to be present

- Preparing meals for your children with knives

- Engaging in arts and crafts with the use of scissors or other items that trigger unwanted thoughts

- Spending time alone with your child or taking him out to a park, for example, and letting the unwanted thoughts join you

- Resisting confessing or seeking reassurance from your partner (or others) about the thoughts and purposefully telling yourself that you are hiding something dangerous

- Allowing children to be unattended when appropriate and accepting thoughts of harm that may befall them

Notice that most of the exposures that are going to be effective for treating your fear of harming children actually amount to simply living your life in accordance with your values, but doing so with the intentional invitation of your unwanted thoughts. Exposures that also have an inherent value (for example, you and your kid made art out of strips of paper you cut with scissors) are going to be both more effective and more likely to be repeated than exposures that simply generate anxiety.

Acceptance and Motivation Scripts

It can be hard to find the motivation to stand up to OCD when you feel completely crushed by it. And again, something about children being involved makes it even more difficult to imagine overcoming. Using an acceptance and motivation script to build up the nerve and get your feet wet may be useful. Start by describing what exposures you're going to do and/or what things you are going to stop avoiding. Then do your best to describe what this really means you are risking. Don't just say "and my child may die," but dig a little deeper into what it is you are afraid might take place because you didn't do your compulsions. Then try to paint a vivid image in words that captures your life completely enslaved by the OCD. Lastly, explore the kind of parent you believe you are (or could become) and how fighting your OCD is the most consistent action with that value.

An Example of an Acceptance and Motivation Script: "I'm going to start being alone with my child again and putting her to bed at night. I am going to allow my harmful thoughts to be there while I do this and I am going to stop confessing to my wife and stop asking her if everything is okay. This may result in me reacting spontaneously to an impulse and throwing my child off the balcony to her death. This could devastate me, my wife, and our extended family, and I could spend the rest of my life in prison or a mental institution. But if I don't make these changes, I am not going to have a relationship with my child. She will only know a father who is avoidant and distant, and will conclude that I don't really love her. I will spend all of my time ruminating on whether or not I am going to harm her and I will never conclude that she is safe. It's worth it to me to stand up to my OCD and demand that my child be mine, not the OCD's. I am an attentive and loving father and if having these thoughts and taking this risk with her is what it takes to be there for my baby, then so be it."

Flooding Scripts

Dark and deep waters lay ahead, so proceed with caution. Remember, flooding scripts are about generating the urge to do compulsions and resisting them. These thoughts are going through your head anyway, but what you are doing in this type of exposure is writing them out and magnifying them with intention. This means getting face to face with the feelings of harm. Use this approach as mortal combat for your OCD.

An Example of a Flooding Script: "I bathe my son in the tub and decide I don't want to be a parent anymore. He looks up at me helplessly, his head resting in my palm. I remove my hand from the back of his head and place it on the front of his face. I push his face under the water. He starts to gasp, then twitches violently. He grabs at my wrist, desperately trying to stop me, but he is too weak. I take my other hand and make sure he can't slip out from under me. He twitches a few more times, then stops. He is dead. I killed him. I drowned my baby. My husband walks in moments later and sees what I've done. He screams and cries and keeps saying 'How could you? What have you done?' I am speechless, dead inside, a zombie. My husband lifts my baby's lifeless body out of the water and tries CPR but it is too late. He calls the police and tells them what happened. When they arrive, they look at me with disgust before taking me to the police station and arresting me."

Still here? That was brutal, I know. You may be feeling sick to your stomach or like you want to jump out of your skin. That's perfectly normal. Remember that those who have this form of OCD are responding to this feeling with compulsions. The purpose of a script like this is to expose oneself to this feeling and to learn how to be better at having it so it doesn't control your behavior.

A: Acceptance and Mindfulness

Children are really good at being in the present. They're also really good at demanding that *you* be in the present, even when you want nothing more than to check out, check your phone, browse through a newspaper, and so on. Developing the skill through mindfulness to actually stay present with children, even when your mind keeps highlighting intrusive thoughts of harming them, is a worthwhile and achievable endeavor.

The first thing to remember about this form of OCD is that the horrible and disgusting "abnormal" thoughts are actually totally normal. The problem has to do with how the thoughts are presented and how they are responded to, not with their existence or absence. The OCD mind is a wide open mind, highlighting extreme potentials in any given context. To cherish something (like a child) is to also be aware of the horror of losing something that you cherish. In other words, as an OCD sufferer, you can't *not* think about this stuff. The problem is that you mistake the simple awareness of this thought for having an intrinsic meaning, instead of just being a mental event that comes with having an OCD mind. Therefore mindfulness, the skill of observing mental events without judgment or analysis, is an essential aspect of mastering the disorder.

The brain records actions much more clearly than thoughts, feelings, or intentions. What this means is that the parent who changes the child's diaper while having intrusive thoughts about committing some vile act in the process is actually recording more helpful information than the parent who is avoiding changing the diaper and the intrusive thoughts. The person who allows the thoughts but not the avoidance is actually programming the brain to perceive the thoughts as irrelevant and the value of the interaction as the most important element. The avoidant person is establishing only that diaper-changing is a threat. One way to keep this concept in mind is to remember that your brain doesn't know that you have OCD and always assumes that your behavior is rational. Therefore, what you avoid is always going to be understood as a danger, whereas what you do exposure to will eventually be understood as nonthreatening.

Developing a more accepting and mindful perspective involves stepping back and opening up to your experience. You can have an unwanted thought and also notice the other details about what is going on. Let yourself view the fearful harming thoughts as just one data stream among many and don't single it out for special attention. Between you and being the mom or dad you want to be is just thoughts and feelings. Let go of resistance to thoughts and feelings and create pathways in the mind that allow the worst of the worst to pass through relatively unnoticed. Then you get the good stuff. The giggles, the hugs, the I-love-you's…and even the unpleasant stuff becomes okay, too. You get back the freedom to be angry without debating in your head what that means, to wake up in the middle of the night to whining and demands and think to yourself, *Man, I'm gonna kill that kid!* without it having to mean anything at all. This freedom is ultimately what allows you to be present with your child.

L: Love and Self-Compassion

Being a parent is hard. It's way harder than people assume it will be before it happens to them. It causes stress, overstimulation, sleep deprivation, and worst of all, the sense that people are watching to see how good you are at it and how good a person you are in general. It may seem as if people care about you more, focus on you more, now that you are responsible for children. And children will press your buttons and try to make you frustrated, because making you *anything* is fascinating to them. But what your children can't understand yet is that if you have OCD and you're stressed, exhausted, frustrated and overstimulated, your disorder flares up. And when your disorder flares up, it targets everything you care about the most and tries to bind it to a living nightmare.

This disorder can trick you into thinking you're the worst of the worst. But you are not the best or worst parent who ever lived. You are just a person with thoughts, feelings, and sensations. Remember, being self-compassionate mostly just means being honest. When you make a mindful statement about fearing harming your children, you are being honest about your experience. When you criticize yourself for having thoughts and for being afraid, you are essentially lying to yourself about what is evident. You have OCD. Commentary about how good a person you are is a distraction from the important work of keeping your OCD from commandeering your family. Similarly, it's important to remember that all healthy parents have "unhealthy" thoughts about their kids and have doubts about their abilities to raise them. They're supposed to. Treating yourself fairly and compassionately is the only rational way to navigate parenthood, with or without having OCD.

An Example of a Coping Statement: "I'm afraid to be left alone with my child because I'm having intrusive thoughts about shooting him. Many people with OCD have these types of thoughts and struggle to be alone with their kids. I'm doing a pretty good job of recognizing my OCD in this moment. I need to give myself permission to be afraid sometimes that my thoughts are dangerous. I can have these feelings and still resist the urge to avoid my son. Maybe I can focus on some activities for us to do together that I will enjoy even if my OCD is giving me a hard time."

You're Not Crazy

Most people say "I'd do anything for my child," but the Harm OCD sufferer has to do more than just show up for the job. You have to show up to this amazing beautiful being even knowing that it aggravates your disorder. You have to do exposure to the darkest, most terrifying corners of the mind. You have to cope with extreme love, often reminding you of extreme fear. You have to tolerate the uncertainty that your child may have a short or painful life in order to maximize the possibility that she has a happy one. To love your children is to be vulnerable to them and to see their vulnerability. You have to risk being harmed and you have to risk harming in order to be close to anyone. OCD can make you think you're too crazy to deserve this closeness with a child. But you're not crazy. You got this.

Recap

H: Have Another Look. The OCD uses cognitive distortions to trick you into thinking you have to do compulsions to keep a child safe. But presence, not perfection, is what makes for good parenting. Challenging distorted assumptions can keep you focused on the most important task of resisting compulsions.

E: Exposure and Response Prevention. Exposures don't put children at risk. What they do is empower you to fight your OCD. It is compulsions that take you away from being the kind of parent you want to be. Removing unnecessary safety behaviors and writing exposure scripts can train you to overcome your fears.

A: Acceptance and Mindfulness. Learning to make space for gruesome and terrifying mental imagery about your kids is no easy feat. However, by practicing staying present with children and with the thoughts that they trigger, you weaken OCD's grip on your attention.

L: Love and Self-Compassion. Recognizing that parenthood is hard and, well, "crazy-making" at times is an important first step in treating yourself with compassion. The better care you take of yourself, the better able you will be to stand up to your OCD when it targets your children.

PART 3

The Bigger Picture

In part 1, I offered an overview of OCD and its relationship to unwanted thoughts about harm and violence, as well as the various treatment approaches you can take to overcome it. In part 2, I went into more depth on some common ways Harm OCD manifests and offered some tips for using the principles of H.E.A.L. In this final section of the book, I will focus on how to maximize your potential for mastery over Harm OCD, including how to get help and how to better help others help you. This part is divided into two chapters, "Harm OCD and Everyone Else," which covers accessing treatment and involving your loved ones, and the concluding chapter, "Harm OCD and You," which focuses on rising above shame and self-stigma for true mastery, with a look at what recovery really is.

CHAPTER 7

Harm OCD and Everyone Else

The problem with thoughts you find repugnant, and learning to cope with them in the most therapeutic way, is that one of your hardest exposures is often the first thing you have to do to get better. In other words, though many people have a variety of obstacles in front of them when seeking professional help (for example, geography, finances, social stigma), those with Harm OCD seeking help are faced with the task of telling another human being the content of their thoughts while simultaneously perceiving that sharing these thoughts could lead to all kinds of actual harm. Harmed if you do, harmed if you don't.

Admitting that you have thoughts about stabbing your infant daughter or that you have thoughts about the possibility that you might have killed a stranger with your car, or that you have thoughts that you may at any moment put a bullet in your head for no reason is, well, not an easy hello. So to begin, offer yourself some respect for the courage it takes to actually give voice to these horrifying thoughts.

Getting Professional Help

The best way to ensure the start of a healthy path is to seek out an evaluation from a mental healthcare provider who specializes in OCD. You can go to https://iocdf.org/find-help/ (the treatment provider page of the International OCD Foundation website) and put in your geographic and other search parameters as one way to locate a potential provider. On that website, you can also find a good list of questions to ask a treatment provider in order to be confident that he or she knows how to evaluate for and treat OCD. Before committing to an appointment, call the person and talk to him or her plainly about what you are experiencing. Something like, "I am having trouble with unwanted intrusive thoughts about harming. I don't want to do anything bad and the thoughts scare me because I worry about what they mean." Let the person you are speaking to ask some clarifying questions. Try your hardest to resist reassurance-seeking right there on the phone.

I do not recommend leading with "I have Harm OCD." Though I and many of my colleagues would immediately know what you mean, many therapists are not trained to label OCD subtypes. This is not necessarily a bad thing. They could be experts in OCD and simply be committing to a more technical clinical description (for example, "OCD with aggressive obsessions"). Subtypes like Harm OCD (and HOCD, ROCD, POCD, and so on) are convenient shorthand, but often lead to unnecessary diagnostic confusion. OCD is obsessive-compulsive disorder. The specific content of your thoughts and the specific rituals you engage in to get certainty about those thoughts is what guides the treatment, not what determines the diagnosis. The diagnosis is determined by the presence of obsessions, compulsions, and impairment.

Some Useful Questions to Ask:

- How much of your practice is made up of OCD patients?

- What treatment approaches do you use? (CBT and ERP are what we're looking for here, not dream analysis)

- Have you ever treated people with unwanted intrusive violent thoughts?

Many OCD specialists do not take insurance and many in-network therapists are not trained in CBT for OCD. But this is not a hard-and-fast rule, so asking questions like those above is worth your time even if the therapist is not calling him- or herself a specialist. If you are seeing a therapist who is not a specialist in OCD, this doesn't mean he won't be able to help you at all. Perhaps he has had some training in CBT for OCD, but his practice simply isn't made up of a majority of OCD patients. That being said, it's reasonable to be skeptical of any therapist's ability to properly assess OCD, particularly when it involves violent obsessions. One study of mental healthcare professionals found that the overall rate of misdiagnosis for taboo thoughts was in fact generally higher than when assessing for contamination obsessions (Glazier et al. 2013). So the more upfront and direct you are about the content of your thoughts and how you experience them, the better able you will be to determine if the person you're speaking to can be helpful with his or her treatment approach.

Arm Yourself With Knowledge, But Don't Weigh Yourself Down

Regardless of what type of treatment provider you decide to see and to what extent they may be a specialist in OCD, it's never too early to start educating yourself on the disorder. This will also help you speak about it with the therapist in a way that gives him or her the most useful information. In addition to reading this book, I recommend checking out several of the books listed at https://iocdf.org/books/. Blogs, online support groups, and YouTube series (for example, *The OCD Stories*) can be useful as well. Before treatment, the OCD knows more about you. It knows how much anxiety and guilt you are willing to tolerate, it knows who you fear harming the most and how, and it knows how to get under your skin and press your buttons. You need to know more about OCD than OCD knows about you.

Just be careful not to use information gathering as a form of compulsive self-reassurance. Knowing where the line separates the two isn't always easy, but one of the biggest pitfalls I see clients struggle with in the early part of their treatment is overresponding to doubt about the diagnosis. For many, hearing that they have OCD is a huge relief because it sounds like they don't have what their OCD keeps saying they have. (Bloodlust? Murderous impulses? A cold heart?) But setting out to be 100% certain that you have OCD can easily become an all-consuming OCD symptom of its own and, at its worst, can interfere in your willingness to take the risk of investing your time, energy, money, and faith in treatment. So yes, read the OCD books and learn from OCD specialists and your fellow sufferers, but don't make needing to know for *certain* that you have Harm OCD into a replacement obsession.

Medication and Harm OCD

Your first interaction with a treatment provider may be a psychiatrist—a medical doctor trained in the diagnosis and treatment of mental disorders. The psychiatrist may recommend medication as part of your overall treatment plan. Though it is clear that certain medications help many people with OCD in some meaningful way, exactly how much of OCD can be explained as a neurochemical problem is unknown. The decision to take medication for OCD may be challenging, but it's important to understand that taking or not taking medication has nothing to do with fighting OCD the easy or hard way. A proper evaluation from a psychiatrist can help you make this determination, but especially for those with more severe symptoms, medication may be an important part of the treatment.

The most commonly prescribed medications in this context are called selective serotonin reuptake inhibitors (SSRIs), and they are typically prescribed at high doses when used to treat OCD (Kellner 2010). In fact, to this date, SSRIs are the only class of medications that have been documented to be effective on their own for OCD, though other medications, such as neuroleptics, may also be used to augment or enhance the effects of these medications (Hirschtritt, Bloch, and Mathews 2017). When effective, medications for OCD can help reduce the intensity of thought intrusion and associated anxiety, making it easier for sufferers to make noncompulsive choices. The key thing to remember here is that with or without medication, it is still *you* making the choice not to do compulsions and to accept uncertainty about your harm thoughts.

Taking medication as part of your treatment for the fear of causing harm can, in and of itself, be a challenging exposure. The OCD will tell you that taking psychiatric medication somehow makes you more of a, well, psychiatric patient, which comes with a type of self-stigma that isn't helpful. Make the determination based on careful consultation with the prescribing doctor, not on subjective assessments of how crazy you think you have to be to get whatever support is available.

For a basic primer on OCD meds, check out https://iocdf.org/about-ocd/treatment/meds/

Harm OCD in Children

This is a book for adults with Harm OCD, but I wanted to include a little information about children with Harm OCD so that any readers who may know of a child with this form of OCD can be supportive. OCD overall affects roughly 1-2% of children (Rapoport et al. 2000). Children who don't have OCD are also grappling with new and sometimes frightening concepts every day in multiple environments, so it should come as no surprise that children who do have OCD can be significantly impaired by their OCD symptoms at home, in school, and in their social life (Piacentini et al. 2003). Given the content of these types of obsessions, one might assume they only occur to adults, but in fact taboo themes of violence, sex, and religious sacrilege frequently come up in pediatric OCD (Masi et al. 2005). Aggressive obsessions may range in prevalence from 32.6-75% of children with OCD (Storch et al. 2008).

If you are a parent reading this, don't worry about whether you caused this by allowing them to play the wrong video game or watch a movie above their maturity level. (Note to self: Ask wife if eight-year-old is ready for *Gremlins.*) OCD is not typically understood to be *caused*, but manifests as a combination of genetic and environmental factors that are not easy to predict. Harm-related thoughts may be especially potent with children because of their general *lack* of exposure to violent concepts and their deficit in being able to make sense of them in an otherwise safe environment. I'm not suggesting that you present a child with material that is not age appropriate, just that you understand that children may struggle with thoughts they have yet to find a place for in their child minds.

Sadly, research indicates that children with Harm OCD tend to be more impaired by their symptoms than children with other obsessions (Storch et al. 2010b). It isn't hard to imagine that many children may avoid disclosing their harm obsessions, both out of shame for having them and out of fear that they will be misinterpreted. It follows, then, that keeping the content of their obsessions to themselves is likely to make the OCD worse, teaching the brain that their symptoms really must be shameful or dangerous. While some may hide their symptoms, other children with Harm OCD may engage in ritualistic reassurance-seeking, desperately trying to draw from others confirmation that these thoughts are just OCD and not signs that they are bad seeds (Wu and Storch 2016). In either case, if you are a parent or other loved one of a child with Harm OCD, remember that normalizing these types of thoughts is an important part of creating a safe place to address them and easing the child's burden.

What Parents Should Know

Violent obsessions in children with OCD often target the parents. After all, the loss of a parent may be the most terrifying thing a child can conjure up. Don't be surprised by the seemingly "grown-up" content of your child's obsessive thoughts. If children know what a knife is, they know what a stab is and the more concern you give the content, the more compulsive they will be with it. Getting your child proper treatment is extremely important and, as discussed above, it is well advised to put in the effort to find an OCD specialist. A child with intrusive violent thoughts may be easily misdiagnosed by a well-meaning therapist unfamiliar with Harm OCD as having been the victim of some kind of physical abuse or exposure to inappropriate material. This can lead to burdening your child with extremely triggering questions about domestic violence or worse, leading to misguided reporting to child protective services.

Treatment of Harm OCD is not meaningfully different with children than with adults. In both, the key is collaborating with the therapist on effective exposures and systematically reducing avoidance and other compulsions. But children with OCD may need more help understanding why this would work, and extra time may need to be taken to get them on board with treatment. Discussing the rationale for exposures may be especially important when treating children with Harm OCD because both the child *and* the parent may fear that ERP is too dangerous or risky (Johnco and Storch 2017).

Disclosing to Family Members and Friends

There are two kinds of people in your life when you have OCD: people who are wrapped up in it and people who aren't. People who are wrapped up in your OCD spend a lot of time with you, witness you doing rituals, take your reassurance-seeking questions and confessions, and generally spend some significant portion of their time trying to keep you from freaking out (usually with only limited success). Sometimes these people are also the ones your OCD says you might end up harming. These people are your partners, your parents, and sometimes your closest friends. These people should take priority when it comes to disclosure of your Harm OCD because these are the ones who are best suited to help you when they have the right information—and also the most likely to make your OCD worse when they have the wrong information.

What you want out of disclosure is someone to truly hear you. It's not about pity (in fact, most people with Harm OCD whom I have encountered seem disgusted by pity). It's about remembering that you are not alone in this universe, but are part of a larger system. Changes you make in your relationship to OCD will bring about changes in the people around you. Changes in the people around you will influence the way you relate to your OCD. Here's a simple way to think about how to disclose when you are asking for a kind *EAR*.

E: Educate

Rather than barrel into "I have Harm OCD and can't stop thinking about murder!" start by educating the person you are disclosing to about OCD in general. You have obsessive-compulsive disorder, a condition where you struggle with unwanted intrusive thoughts and get stuck in a loop when you try to get rid of them. Share some information about the disorder from an article or book on the subject. Set a solid platform of understanding about OCD before going on to the next phase of disclosure.

A: Articulate

Now that your trusted collaborator is thinking about you in the context of having OCD, you can get more specific about the content of your thoughts. This is, of course, especially useful to treatment providers because they will be collaborating with you on the most effective exposures for treating your obsession. With loved ones, articulating the content may be less important. However, it may be helpful to at least articulate some of it so that they understand why you seem to get triggered in some observable situations and not others (for example, while watching the news). Consider that by doing this, you give yourself a little bit of a buffer from questions they may ask that you'd rather not answer in the middle of an anxiety attack.

R: Recommend

Once you've educated them on OCD and articulated your unique experience of having OCD, you can recommend strategies that they can employ to help you. Helping you doesn't always mean helping you with treatment or exposures. It can also mean giving you space when you need it. For a more comprehensive exploration of the issue, you might encourage them to read *When a Family Member Has OCD* (Hershfield 2015).

Don't expect to immediately feel better after disclosure. For many, disclosing is like donating a kidney. Sure, it's for a good cause, but the recovery can be pretty painful. You may feel particularly vulnerable with your "secret" out. No matter how gracefully people receive your disclosure, don't be surprised when self-criticism and shame roll in. Your OCD may tell you that you've made a terrible mistake or that people think horrible things about you. Get ready to implement some heavy self-compassion strategies in response. It's worth it in the long run. When you avoid disclosure in situations where it would really benefit you, that shame train still arrives right on time. The pain you think you're avoiding just gets turned inward and creates more self-doubt and self-judgment in the end.

How Your Family Can Help

Getting others on board can be instrumental in overcoming Harm OCD. The two best things a family member (or any trusted love one) can do to help you with your Harm OCD is to stop reassuring you and to stop facilitating avoidance. Of course, this all depends on you and your willingness to invite them to do this. What needs to be done is for you to form an alliance with others against the OCD. The OCD tries to drive a wedge between you and the other people in your system, tries to isolate you in order to maximize its bullying. With others on board with you against the OCD, you stand a better chance. This way, if the OCD tricks you into asking for reassurance, your loved one can be there to correct the experience. "Sorry, that sounds like reassurance. Can't answer."

"Contracts" are particularly useful, with or without the guidance of a therapist. If you can articulate how your loved ones can help you resist compulsions, and they can understand this, it's helpful to have an actual document to refer to where this is laid out. In terms of reassurance, you can collaborate with your family members on the best ways to reply when you are having a difficult time resisting asking those compulsive questions.

SAMPLE REASSURANCE CONTRACT:

My OCD makes me worry a lot about harming. To make myself feel safe from harming, I may try to ask you to reassure me that I would not commit harm. Though it will make me feel better in the short term to hear you say something reassuring, this only strengthens my OCD. Instead of reassuring me, I want you to tell me that you won't answer my questions about harming and that you're standing with me in my struggle against OCD.

You can modify this however you see fit, including additional recommendations for how your family members can deny or interfere in your reassurance-seeking. You probably don't want untrained family members pretending to be your therapist and throwing exposure opportunities at you randomly. But they can still discourage your avoidance by repeatedly inviting you to participate in activities they would otherwise be doing (including cooking with knives, watching that show with all the gun scenes, or taking that hike down the secluded trail where their murdered body is unlikely to be found). Loving someone is learning to be just a *little* okay with the possibility of killing them. Otherwise you won't spend enough time at harming distance to know what true love is.

Except for That One

Let's be perfectly honest, not everyone in your system is adept at contributing positively to it. We all have our own issues and sometimes another person's issues may get in the way of supporting you in yours. Use your best judgment to assess the people you care about for their competency to support before asking them to handle this delicate material. This doesn't mean you have to cut anyone out of your life, but only you know who is likely to be a good part of your support team and who is likely to make things worse. Some qualities to look out for might be a tendency to overreact, to categorically reject mental health issues, to change stories about you into stories about them, and above all, any history of using your personal information to shame you. You don't need more of that.

Disclosing to Anyone

The important thing to remember about disclosing Harm OCD is that what you see in your mind is different from what other people see in their minds when they hear about it. When you have Harm OCD, you feel as if you are *in* the horror movie. But to everyone else, a description of unwanted harm thoughts is just a screenplay of that horror movie. The content you describe may or may not accurately depict what you're thinking, but even if the image that comes up in the mind of the person you're disclosing to is *worse* than what you are trying to describe, the interpretation of that image is likely less impressive.

Consider how *you* feel about other people's obsessions. You struggle with unwanted violent thoughts, so what do you really think about people who obsess primarily about germs? You probably have empathy for them, but imagine that it can't really be that bad. *I mean, it's not violence, right? If you get sick, you get sick, but if you kill a school bus full of children*…Okay, that escalated quickly.

So this is the double-edged sword of disclosure. The people you are disclosing to are unlikely to fully appreciate the pain you are in because they just can't imagine taking thoughts like these as seriously as you do. On the other hand, this also means that the average person is unlikely to overvalue your unwanted thoughts and judge you harshly or think of you as a horrible person for having the thoughts.

So Why Tell Anyone?

First, it's important to consider that *anything* you do to treat harm thoughts as somehow different from the other nonsense in the mind leads the brain to conclude that harm thoughts are special. We don't want harm thoughts to be special. So if you are a person who typically shares meaningful truths about your life experience with people, but go out of your way to keep only *these* types of thoughts a deep, dark secret, you feed the OCD's lie about the special nature of harm thoughts. Remember, the way you overcome any kind of OCD is by learning to treat your thoughts as simply thoughts and being willing to live with uncertainty about their meaning. So disclosing your Harm OCD in some circumstances can be looked at as a type of exposure, not just because it's scary, but because it helps you practice treating the thoughts like they are less special. Of course, when I speak of disclosure, I am not referring to compulsive confessing of your thoughts aimed at getting reassurance. Instead, I mean sharing knowledge about your condition, your inner world, with people of your choosing.

You're Not Crazy

Whether you have intrusive thoughts of harming other people or of harming yourself, your mental health affects those around you. Therapists who do CBT are there to help, medication is there to help, and individuals in your family system are there to help, too. But reaching out for help from any of the above requires courage. I'm not going to lie to you right here and say that everyone gets it, because they don't. Not everybody understands you and your Harm OCD, but that's not because you're crazy. It's because they are uneducated. Educating yourself is the first step toward educating others and building a team of support. This is the fight of your life, so never forget that anything you do to defy the OCD, including reaching out for help, is a power move, not a sign of weakness.

Recap

- Reaching out for help isn't always easy, but finding the right treatment provider can be important. Medication isn't for everyone, but it can be a useful tool in managing your symptoms.

- Harm OCD can manifest in children even though the content of violent thoughts can seem very mature.

- Disclosing to loved ones and soliciting their support can be a valuable part of your treatment, and using the principals of EAR (Educate, Articulate, and Recommend) may help.

CHAPTER 8

Harm OCD and You

How long were you experiencing OCD symptoms before you picked up this book? Six months? A year? Five years? Well, if you're beating yourself up for not looking for help sooner, you're not alone. The average span of time between onset of symptoms and actually getting help for OCD is over ten years (Grant et al. 2006). The number-one reason why people put off getting help is that they are ashamed of the intrusive thoughts. If you struggle with moral obsessions, including Harm OCD, you may be more affected by shame and fear of being stigmatized than those who struggle with other types of obsessions because you may fear being looked at by treatment providers (or others) as deviant (Glazier et al. 2015). I wanted to end this book with a discussion about shame, because learning to step through shame is the most powerful tool you can develop for mastering Harm OCD. Why? Because as it turns out, the strongest predictor of quality of life with OCD is not how bad your OCD symptoms are. It's how much shame you experience having OCD (Singh et al. 2016).

Shame and Harm OCD

So what is this thing, shame? Shame can be understood as a negative assessment of your whole self, as opposed to a negative assessment only of something you did. Guilt is "I did something bad," while shame is "I am bad." In some studies, roughly half of those diagnosed with

OCD reported shame for having it and shame for needing help (Williams et al. 2011).

Throughout this book, I have focused primarily on the fear of causing harm and the guilt that people with Harm OCD have over these intrusive thoughts and imagine they would have if their thoughts came true. However, to truly tackle Harm OCD, it's important to recognize the role that shame plays as well. When you struggle with unwanted thoughts of violence, you may also struggle with unwanted thoughts about who you are in the first place. Who thinks this way? What kind of person am I that I think this way?

TAF + Shame = More Compulsions

As discussed in chapter 2's list of cognitive distortions, believing that having a thought is akin to doing a bad thing—a distorted way of thinking that confuses mental behaviors with actual ones—is called thought-action fusion (TAF) (Shafran, Thordardson, and Rachman 1996). If you struggle with this thinking error, you may have come to believe that having the intrusive thoughts implies something bad about your moral character (TAF-morality). One study found that if people are prone to experiencing shame, struggling with TAF-morality means that they are more likely to engage in compulsions (Valentiner and Smith 2008). Take a moment to consider what this really means. Your brain tricks you into thinking that having a "bad" thought is the same as doing a bad thing (thought-action fusion) and you may already be wired for this to be viewed in terms of morality (TAF-morality). So you have an unwanted violent thought and you feel as if you've already committed an immoral act simply by having the thought. If you are also a person who is likely to condemn your whole character for being imperfect, then the thought/perceived act becomes a shame-producer. Compulsions, therefore, are strategies for escaping the severe emotional pain of shame. So learning to be shame-resilient is a smart way to take away Harm OCD's sharpest weapon.

Shame Resilience and Mindfulness

Brene Brown defines shame resilience in her book *Daring Greatly* as "the ability to practice authenticity when we experience shame, to move through the experience without sacrificing our values, and to come out on the other side of the shame experience with more courage, compassion and connection than we had going into it" (2012, 74). In Harm OCD terms, this means establishing within yourself a willingness to be in the presence of shame as it arises in response to your decision not to do compulsions, to be willing to experience the shame as it is, and then to be a witness to the benefits of having done your exposure.

Shame becomes toxic when you buy into it, when you convince yourself that you are bad. So naturally we want to avoid shame, even in doing ERP. But when you see shame for what it is—thoughts and feelings about being bad, objects of attention—then it doesn't have to be a barrier to effective ERP. Mindfulness, then, becomes a way to see shame arising in the course of doing ERP and to know that it is not proof of your inadequacy, but just a reaction to thoughts and feelings. Mindfulness allows you to widen the space in which these thoughts and feelings exist. When we imagine that we cannot tolerate a thought or feeling, we imagine it as a large object in a small space about to burst. But when we widen our perspective, we recognize that there is unlimited space and these objects of our attention seem smaller and smaller. This doesn't mean analyzing or "thinking" about them, but simply letting ourselves experience them, as they are, without judgment.

Mindfulness is not a thing that "works" or "doesn't work." To view mindfulness as a trick for getting rid of thoughts and feelings is to miss the point. Being awake doesn't work or not work. It is simply a way of being. You may be tired (less awake) or wired (very awake), but it remains a state of being, not an activity. Mindfulness is not a hammer or a screwdriver. Mindfulness is an understanding of how things are built.

Your Character Is Unique, But Not an Antique

If you've had Harm OCD for a long time, you've been carrying around your moral character like it's a very expensive antique. The thing about expensive antiques is that they can only take a little wear and tear before their perceived financial value plummets dramatically. One might assume that simply doing all the right things just the right way (the way OCD says you have to) will keep this precious antique in mint condition. But this is nonsense. Life is hard. Really hard. Even the easy parts. So this thing you carry around is going to get dented and scratched, and you need to love it anyway.

If you've had Harm OCD for a long time and have either never been treated or have struggled to find an effective treatment, you may have come to some of the following false conclusions:

- I'm not better because I don't really have Harm OCD, I'm just damaged goods.

- I had my chance to get better and now that ship has sailed.

- I don't deserve to get better.

- I should have gotten better earlier.

- I am too far gone with these thoughts to ever be free.

- I failed when I started thinking these thoughts and all I've done is fail since.

- There's no point to recognizing my good qualities when I am a bad person.

These are just a few of the shame-based comments I've heard in my time working with Harm OCD sufferers. The OCD has been telling you for so long that you are going to hurt someone (including yourself), that you can't imagine being happy. Nor can you imagine that you are messed up like everyone else. No, you believe you're a *special* kind of messed up that no one wants to talk about. This way of thinking is actually part of the disorder. Happiness is not something one deserves or doesn't deserve. It's freely available to anyone who wishes to reach out and grab it. But you have to be willing to start now. You don't get to rewrite the past. You don't get to scrub the history of thinking horrible thoughts and then start from scratch. You start now. This moment. And now again. This moment. Take a moment to recognize that you are currently reading a book about overcoming your Harm OCD. You are already inside the process of overcoming your OCD challenges and you're already further along than the first step.

What Does It Really Look Like to Overcome Harm OCD?

Overcoming any form of OCD may look different to different sufferers, but one thing remains the same—intrusive thoughts are part of life. If you're imagining overcoming Harm OCD as something like never having another unwanted violent thought or never experiencing any anxiety, then you're still playing by the OCD's rules and still being an active participant in your own suffering. It's natural to have unwanted thoughts (yes, even repugnant violent ones) and it's natural to experience occasional anxiety (yes, even when nothing is actually wrong). Mastering OCD means living with little or no impairment, but also means being ready for the fight when OCD flares up. This may involve being in therapy and/or taking medication indefinitely, sporadically, or not at all. Your journey is your journey.

Below is a glimpse at what Harm OCD sufferers could look like when they become Harm OCD masters. I've included just a few bullet points that indicate their progress in freeing themselves from OCD. Consider what other indicators of mastery might be found in the following characters that were introduced at the beginning of the book.

Joanna

Joanna spent a lot of time ruminating over whether she was a bad person because she often thought she might not have been vigilant enough in keeping others safe. She even suspected that she might have violent intentions toward others and could be some sort of sociopath who willingly allows people to get harmed. What are some ways we would know if she got better?

- *She stopped reading articles about serial killers to prove she wasn't one and started watching serial killer detective shows and letting herself just enjoy them. When asked how she could tolerate the violence in the British detective show Luther, all she could think to say was, "Idris Elba is ridiculously good looking."*

- *She challenged herself daily to resist seeking certainty whenever she had the thought that she might have let someone get harmed. She got in the habit of saying to herself, "Not everyone gets to live" whenever she considered confessing to her husband that she forgot to wash her hands after taking out the trash.*

- *She meditated daily and learned to observe her self-critical thoughts as part of the larger stream of thoughts in her consciousness. She began to view treating herself with disdain as a form of harming the people who love her. She began to view questions about whether she "cared enough" about the safety of others as challenges to care less.*

Mandy

Mandy's Harm OCD was triggered by news of a violent event. She worried that her intrusive violent thoughts could lead to her snapping and harming someone. This led to years and years of desperately trying to avoid anything that might trigger the thoughts. What would be some indicators that she got better?

- She stopped avoiding people she cared about even when her OCD told her she might hurt them, and instead took the opportunity to practice ERP and demand more closeness with her loved ones.

- She started using knives in the kitchen and actually became a pretty good cook. After washing the knives she used, she would just leave them out on a towel to dry.

- She practiced ERP, sometimes every day, sometimes whenever she needed it. On days when her OCD seemed to be in high gear, she wrote scripts about snapping and slept with a knife by her bed. For every three romantic comedies she made her husband watch, she made sure to select one movie she thought might be triggering.

- She still continued to see her therapist, sometimes weekly, sometimes going months between sessions. When she talked about her intrusive thoughts, she spoke plainly about them like they were symptoms of a cold and she resisted urges to ask her therapist for reassurance.

Elizabeth

Elizabeth had intrusive fears of committing suicide even though she did not feel suicidal herself. Her OCD told her that she could jump from a ledge at any moment and this led to avoidance and other compulsions. What are some ways we would know that she's developed some mastery over her OCD?

- She was able to get a room in a hotel without insisting it be on a lower floor, and would even ask for the room with the best view of the city.

- She consistently responded to intrusive thoughts with humor and a shrug. She stopped trying to convince herself she was safe *because she had things she loved in life and instead just loved the things in her life.*

- *Her triggering thoughts flared up from time to time, especially around stressful events, but she reminded her husband not to reassure her during these times and not to let her avoid the household cleaners or medicine cabinet.*

- *She practiced mindfulness and used ERP when thoughts got sticky. She knows all the lyrics to Nevermind by Nirvana.*

Richard

Richard's Harm OCD told him he was going to shoot his infant child with a gun, despite the fact that he hated guns and loved his son. He tried to prove he could never do it by avoiding anything gun-related and he severely limited any alone time with his son for fear that he would act out. What would indicate his recovery?

- *He frequently went out of his way to spend time alone with his son and let the thoughts do as they pleased.*

- *He went to a shooting range and took lessons in using a firearm (even though he still doesn't own a gun, it's just not his thing).*

- *He practiced ERP by going to sporting goods stores and watching movies with lots of shootouts.*

- *He still writes the occasional script about losing it and assassinating the poor boy. Sometimes he does this in his head with his son right there, but not to check for self-reassurance.*

Everyone with Harm OCD has the capacity to learn to be something greater than his or her unwanted thoughts. One day you'll look back on this phase of your life, this living nightmare where you devoted so much attention to trying to be certain you would never harm yourself or anyone else, and remember, "Wow, that was a really hard time." Yes, you'll still get a kick in the gut now and again. Stress, sleep deprivation, or just being alive on earth will occasionally cause the OCD to rear its ugly head and take a swipe at you when it can. There will be lapses and occasional relapses that may require some hard work to recover from. See *Everyday Mindfulness for OCD* (Hershfield and Nicely 2017) for tips on navigating these bumps in the road. But if you learn to use your ERP and mindfulness skills as a consistent part of your lifestyle, you can free your attention for the people and things you really care about.

Take the opportunity now to write out a short list of things that would indicate that *you've* developed mastery over your Harm OCD. You may be just starting out or well into the therapeutic process, but ask yourself, "What would it look like to me?" How do you imagine your relationship with Harm OCD getting better? Notice urges to say things like "I'll stop having harm thoughts" and try to redirect yourself to something more realistic and more meaningful. What role will unwanted violent thoughts play in your life? What things do you care about that you will enjoy again?

You're Really Not Crazy

As we approach the finish line of this book, I encourage you to consider one not-so-subtle way your Harm OCD may be holding you back. Harm OCD leads you to believe that you are going to do something terrible, that you've done something terrible, or that you yourself are something terrible. You may have found, then, that when you strive to do something great, something that may get you noticed by others, you suddenly become aware of the idea that your intrusive thoughts could ruin it.

For example, what if you become president and then spontaneously harm yourself or someone else like your OCD says? Or what if it's discovered that you somehow harmed someone in your past and now it is coming to light? Could there be a hashtag with your name on it just waiting to reveal itself at the moment you achieve your hopes and dreams? The OCD is going to make it seem as if falling from a low place is more sensible than falling from a high place, but this is a trap. The OCD is trying to get you to do the worst avoidance compulsion of all, avoidance of leading a fulfilling life. The concern is that your fall from grace will include some kind of public humiliation and that this will inevitably cause tremendous harm to people around you. In other words, if your fears come true when you're president, not only will your character be assassinated, but your loved ones, colleagues, and all the people who voted for you will suffer too.

So how can we do exposure to this one? As it turns out, pretty much all ERP for all Harm OCD begins and ends with this: choosing to live your life. When you start to let go of safety behaviors, such as by putting the kitchen knives back where they belong, you also begin to cook again. When you get behind the wheel of the car and let thoughts of turning into oncoming traffic come and go, you also begin to visit friends again. When you spend time alone with your sweet, innocent loved one and take the risk that some secret monster version of you will lash out, you also begin to access affection again. But this is only the beginning. Reclaiming what you've lost to your Harm OCD goes beyond a return to the activities you once enjoyed and the people you once enjoyed sharing them with. Truly standing up to Harm OCD is to go after a bigger life than the one you had before.

You don't have to aim to be the leader of the free world, but I recommend that you aim higher than your self-doubt. Sure, anyone could aspire to maximize their potential as a human being, but that's not what I'm emphasizing here. What I'm advocating is sticking it to the OCD by flaunting how much you are capable of when you allow yourself to accept uncertainty about your intrusive thoughts. Don't just get by. Take your fear of harming to wherever harming would do the most damage. Taunt the OCD by letting people know you, by starting a family, by marketing yourself professionally, and so on. Take every opportunity you can to tell the OCD, "If you're going to ruin my life, you're going to have a lot to ruin. I'd like to see you try."

Acknowledgments

I want to thank Jess O'Brien for remembering I wanted to write a book on Harm OCD, and the rest of the team at New Harbinger for reining in my sick sense of humor and tendency to drone on and sort of dance around the point and mix metaphors and write run-on sentences like this one you are reading right now. I also want to thank my patient wife for listening to me complain about deadlines and my equally patient kids for tolerating my working on this on weekends. Additional thanks to Jonathan Grayson for agreeing to write the Foreword even after telling me multiple times that he doesn't write forewords; to Eric Storch for generously sharing some of his research when I started this book; and to Shala Nicely for being on the receiving end of many desperate texts about the book not meeting my OCD's expectations.

References

Aardema, F., and K. O'Connor. 2007. "The Menace Within: Obsessions and the Self." *Journal of Cognitive Psychotherapy* 21: 182-197.

Abramowitz, J. S., M. E. Franklin, S. A. Schwartz, and J. M. Furr. 2003a. "Symptom Presentation and Outcome of Cognitive-Behavioral Therapy for Obsessive-Compulsive Disorder." *Journal of Consulting and Clinical Psychology* 71: 1049-1057.

Abramowitz, J. S., S. A. Schwartz, K. M. Moore, and K. R. Luenzmann. 2003b. "Obsessive-Compulsive Symptoms in Pregnancy and the Puerperium: A Review of the Literature." *Journal of Anxiety Disorders* 17: 461-478.

Abramowitz, J. S., B. J. Deacon, B. O. Olatunji, M. G. Wheaton, N. C. Berman, D. Losardo, K. Timpano, P. McGrath, B. Riemann, T. Adams, T. Björgvinsson, E. Storch, and L. R. Hale. 2010. "Assessment of Obsessive-Compulsive Symptom Dimensions: Development and Evaluation of the Dimensional Obsessive-Compulsive Scale." *Psychological Assessment* 22: 180-198.

American Psychiatric Association [APA]. 2013. *Diagnostic and Statistical Manual of Mental Disorders, Fifth Edition [DSM-V]*. Arlington, VA: American Psychiatric Assocation.

Baer, L. 2001. *Imp of the Mind*. New York: Penguin.

Booth, B. D., S. H. Friedman, S. Curry, H. Ward, and S. Stewart. 2014. "Obsessions of Child Murder: Underrecognized Manifestations of Obsessive-Compulsive Disorder." *Journal of the American Academy of Psychiatry and the Law* 42: 66-74.

Brown, B. 2012. *Daring Greatly*. New York: Avery.

Burns, D. D. 1989. *The Feeling Good Handbook: Using the New Mood Therapy in Everyday Life*. New York: W. Morrow.

Ching, T. H. W., M. Williams, and J. Siev. 2017. "Violent Obsessions Are Associated with Suicidality in an OCD Analog Sample of College Students." *Cognitive Behaviour Therapy* 46: 129-140.

Craske, M. G., K. Kircanski, M. Zelikowski, J. Mystkowsi, N. Chowdhury, and A. Baker. 2008. "Optimizing Inhibitory Learning During Exposure Therapy." *Behaviour Research and Therapy* 46: 5-27.

Glazier, K., R. M. Calixte, R. Rothschild, and A. Pinto. 2013. "High Rates of OCD Symptom Misidentification by Mental Health Professionals." *Annals of Clinical Psychiatry* 25: 201-209.

Glazier, K., C. T. Wetterneck, S. Singh, and M. T. Williams. 2015. "Stigma and Shame as Barriers to Treatment in Obsessive-Compulsive and Related Disorders." *Journal of Depression and Anxiety* 4: 191.

Golden, A., W. Haynes, M. VanDyke, and C. Pollard. 2016. "Treatment of Aggressive Obsessions in an Adult with Obsessive-Compulsive Disorder." In Storch E., Lewin A. (eds) *Clinical Handbook of Obsessive-Compulsive and Related Disorders*, edited by Eric A. Storch and Adam B. Lewin. Switzerland: Springer.

Goodman, W., L. H. Price, S. A. Rasmussen, C. Mazure, R. L. Fleischmann, C. L. Hill, and D. Charney. 1989. "The Yale-Brown Obsessive Compulsive Scale Part I: Development, Use and Reliability." *Archives of General Psychiatry* 46: 1006-1011.

Grant, J. E., A. Pinto, M. Gunnip, M. C. Mancebo, J. L. Eisen, et al. 2006. "Sexual Obsessions and Clinical Correlates in Adults with Obsessive-Compulsive Disorder. *Comprehensive Psychiatry* 47: 325-329.

Grayson, J. 2003. *Freedom from Obsessive Compulsive Disorder.* New York: Berkley Books.

Hershfield, J. 2015. *When a Family Member Has OCD: Mindfulness and Cognitive Behavioral Skills to Help Families Affected by Obsessive-Compulsive Disorder.* Oakland, CA: New Harbinger Publications.

Hershfield, J., and T. Corboy. 2013. *The Mindfulness Workbook for OCD: A Guide to Overcoming Obsessions and Compulsions Using Mindfulness and Cognitive Behavioral Therapy.* Oakland, CA: New Harbinger Publications.

Hershfield, J., and S. Nicely. 2017. *Everyday Mindfulness for OCD: Tips, Tricks, and Skills for Living Joyfully.* Oakland, CA: New Harbinger Publications.

Hirschtritt, M. E., M. H. Bloch, and C. A. Mathews. 2017. "Obsessive-Compulsive Disorder: Advances in Diagnosis and Treatment." *Journal of the American Medical Association* 317: 1358-1367.

Jacoby, R. J., and J. S. Abramowitz. 2016. "Inhibitory Learning Approaches to Exposure Therapy: A Critical Review and Translation to Obsessive-Compulsive Disorder." *Clinical Psychology Review* 49: 28-40.

Jacoby, R., R. Leonard, B. Riemann, and J. Abramowitz. 2016. "Self-Punishment as a Maladaptive Thought Control Strategy Mediates the Relationship Between Beliefs About Thoughts and Repugnant Obsessions." *Cognitive Therapy and Research* 40: 179-187.

Johnco, C., and E. A. Storch. 2017. "Unacceptable Obsessional Thoughts in Children and Adolescents." In *The Wiley Handbook of Obsessive Compulsive Disorders*, edited by Jonathan S. Abramowitz, Dean McKay, and Eric A. Storch. Chichester, UK: John Wiley and Sons.

Kellner, M. 2010. "Drug Treatment of Obsessive-Compulsive Disorder." *Dialogues in Clinical Neuroscience* 12: 187-197.

Lee, H. J., and S. M. Kwon. 2003. "Two Different Types of Obsessions: Autogenous Obsessions and Reactive Obsessions. *Behavior Research and Therapy* 41: 11-29.

Lee, E. B., S. Bistricky, A. Milam, C. T. Wetterneck, and T. Björgvinsson. 2016. "Thought Control Strategies and Symptom Dimensions in Obsessive-Compulsive Disorder: Associations With Treatment Outcome." *Journal of Cognitive Psychotherapy* 30: 177-189.

Leonard, R., and B. Riemann. 2012. "The Co-occurrence of Obsessions and Compulsions in OCD." *Journal of Obsessive-Compulsive and Related Disorders* 1: 211-215.

Masi, G., S. Millepiedi, M. Mucci, N. Bertini, L. Milantoni, and F. Arcangeli. 2005. "A Naturalistic Study of Referred Children and Adolescents with Obsessive-Compulsive Disorder." *Journal of the American Academy of Child and Adolescent Psychiatry* 44: 673-681.

Moulding, R., F. Aardema, and K. P. O'Connor. 2014. "Repugnant Obsessions: A Review of the Phenomenology, Theoretical Models, and Treatment of Sexual and Aggressive Obsessional Themes in OCD." *Journal of Obsessive-Compulsive and Related Disorder* 3: 161-168.

Neff, K. 2011. *Self-Compassion: Stop Beating Yourself Up and Leave Insecurity Behind.* New York: William Morrow.

Piacentini, J., R. L. Bergman, M. Keller, and J. McCracken. 2003. "Functional Impairment in hildren and Adolescents with Obsessive-Compulsive Disorder. *Journal of Child and Adolescent Psychopharmacology* 13: S61-S69.

Pinker, S. 2011. *The Better Angels of Our Nature.* New York: Viking.

Purdon, C. 2004. "Cognitive-Behavioral Treatment of Repugnant Obsessions." *Journal of Clinical Psychology* 60: 1169-1180.

Rachman, S., and P. de Silva. 1978. "Abnormal and Normal Obsessions." *Behaviour Research and Therapy* 16: 233-248.

Rachman, S., and R. Shafran. 1999. "Cognitive Distortions: Thought–Action Fusion." *Clinical Psychology and Psychotherapy* 6: 80-85.

Rapoport, J. L., G. Inoff-Germain, M. M. Weissman, S. Greenwald, W. E. Narrow, P. S. Jensen, B. B. Lahey, and G. Canino. 2000. "Childhood Obsessive-Compulsive Disorder in the NIMH MECA Study: Parent Versus Child Identification of Cases." *Journal of Anxiety Disorders* 14: 535-548.

Rasmussen, S. A., and M. T. Tsuang. 1986. "Clinical Characteristics and Family History in DSM-III Obsessive-Compulsive Disorder." *American Journal of Psychiatry* 143: 317-322.

Rasmussen, S. A., and J. L. Eisen. 1992. The Epidemiology and Clinical Features of Obsessive Compulsive Disorder. *Psychiatric Clinics of North America* 15: 743-758.

Riskind, J. H., C. R. Ayers, and E. Wright. 2007. "Simulated Interpersonal Provocation and Fears of a Loss of Impulse Control as Determinants of Aggressive Mental Intrusions." *Journal of Cognitive Psychotherapy* 21: 285-294.

Ruscio, A. M., D. J. Stein, W. T. Chiu, and R. C. Kessler. 2010. "The Epidemiology of Obsessive-Compulsive Disorder in the National Comorbidity Survey Replication." *Molecular Psychiatry* 15: 53-63.

Scahill, L., M. A. Riddle, M. McSwiggin-Hardin, S. I. Ort, R. A. King, W. K. Goodman, D. Cicchetti, and J. F. Leckmna. 1997. "Children's Yale-Brown Obsessive Compulsive Scale: Reliability and Validity." *Journal of the American Academy of Child and Adolescent Psychiatry* 36: 844-852.

Shafran, R., D. S. Thordardson, and S. Rachman. 1996. "Thought-Action Fusion in Obsessive-Compulsive Disorder." *Journal of Anxiety Disorders* 10: 379-391.

Singh, R., C. T. Wetterneck, M. T. Williams, and L. E. Knott. 2016. "The Role of Shame and Symptom Severity on Quality of Life in Obsessive-Compulsive and Related Disorders." *Journal of Obsessive Compulsive and Related Disorders* 11: 49-55.

Storch, E. A., C. W. Lack, L. J. Merlo, G. R. Geffken, M. L. Jacob, T. K. Murphy, and W. K. Goodman. 2007. "Clinical Features of Children and Adolescents with Obsessive-Compulsive Disorder and Hoarding Symptoms." *Comprehensive Psychiatry* 48: 313-318.

Storch, E. A., L. J. Merlo, M. J. Larson, C. S. Bloss, G. R. Geffken, M. L. Jacob, and W. K. Goodman. 2008. "Symptom Dimensions and Cognitive-Behavioural Therapy Outcome for Pediatric Obsessive-Compulsive Disorder." *Acta Psychiatrica Scandinavica* 117: 67-75.

Storch, E. A., M. J. Larson, W. K. Goodman, S. A. Rasmussen, L. H. Price, and T. K. Murphy. 2010a. "Development and Psychometric Evaluation of the Yale-Brown Obsessive Compulsive Scale—Second Edition." *Psychological Assessment* 22: 223-232.

Storch, E. A., T. Björgvinsson, B. Riemann, A. B. Lewin, M. J. Morales, and T. K. Murphy. 2010b. "Factors Associated with Poor Response in Cognitive-Behavioral Therapy for Pediatric Obsessive-Compulsive Disorder." *Bulletin of the Menninger Clinic* 74: 167-185.

Valentiner, D. P., and S. A. Smith. 2008. "Believing That Intrusive Thoughts Can Be Immoral Moderates the Relationship Between Obsessions and Compulsions for Shame-Prone Individuals." *Cognitive Therapy and Research* 32: 714-720.

Wegner, D. M. 1989. *White Bears and Other Unwanted Thoughts: Suppression, Obsession, and the Psychology of Mental Control.* New York: Viking/Penguin.

Wetterneck, C.T., S. Singh, and J. Hart. 2014. "Shame Proneness in Symptom Dimensions of Obsessive-Compulsive Disorder." *Bulletin of the Menninger Clinic* 78: 177-190.

Williams, M. T., S. G. Farris, E. Turkheimer, A. Pinto, K. Ozanick, M. E. Franklin, M. Liebowitz, H. B. Simpson, and E. B. Foa. 2011. "Myth of the Pure Obsessional Type in Obsessive-Compulsive Disorder." *Depression and Anxiety* 28: 495-500.

Winston, S. M., and M. N. Seif. 2017. *Overcoming Unwanted Intrusive Thoughts.* Oakland, CA: New Harbinger Publications.

Wu, M. S., and E. A. Storch. 2016. "A Case Report of Harm-Related Obsessions in Pediatric Obsessive-Compulsive Disorder." *Journal of Clinical Psychology* 72: 1120-1128.

Jon Hershfield, MFT, is director of The OCD and Anxiety Center of Greater Baltimore in Hunt Valley, MD. He specializes in the use of mindfulness and cognitive behavioral therapy (CBT) for obsessive-compulsive disorder (OCD) and related disorders. He is author of *When a Family Member Has OCD*, and coauthor of *The Mindfulness Workbook for OCD* and *Everyday Mindfulness For OCD*.

Foreword writer **Jonathan Grayson, PhD**, is a licensed psychologist specializing in OCD, director of the Grayson Center, and adjunct clinical assistant professor of psychiatry and behavioral sciences at the University of Southern California, where he lectures and supervises residents.

MORE BOOKS *from*
NEW HARBINGER PUBLICATIONS

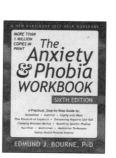